New Environments for Working

The re-design of offices and environmental systems
for new ways of working

Andrew Laing
Francis Duffy
Denice Jaunzens
Steve Willis

BRE   DEGW
Garston   Porters North
Watford   8 Crinan Street
WD2 7JR   London N19SQ

Contents

Part 4: Case studies

Part 5: Product directions and design implications

Bibliography and appendices

Sponsors of the research

The New Environments for Working study was a collaboration between DEGW International Consulting Limited and BRE Ltd. The project team wish to acknowledge the support of the Department of the Environment, Transport and the Regions through their funding of the Partners in Technology programme, and the generous support offered by the following corporate sponsors:

Arenson/President
Hammerson
Interior
Johnson Controls
Land Securities
National Power
SAS Group
Thorn Lighting Group

List of contributors

Dr Francis Duffy CBE, Founder and Chairman of the international architectural and consultancy practice DEGW, is Past President of the RIBA and one of the leading thinkers and practitioners in the science of workplace design.

Dr Andrew Laing is Director of Research at DEGW International Consulting Limited, where he specialises in leading multi-client funded research projects focused on the impact of users' changing needs for the office workplace.

Denice Jaunzens is a senior researcher in the Indoor Environment Division at BRE. Her interests lie in the low energy integrated design of building services and architecture.

Stephen Willis who, whilst at BRE, was responsible for many of the original ideas which underpin this project.

Jon Wilkins, formerly of BRE, is now an operational researcher for the Post Office.

Nigel Oseland is a senior researcher in the Indoor Environment Divison at BRE. He is an expert in the fields of thermal comfort and productivity of office workers.

Anthony Slater is head of the BRE Building Services Centre, specialising in lighting control issues.

Robert Worden, a former Senior Consultant of Logica UK Limited.

Alan Couzens is a Senior Consultant within the Consulting Business Unit of Johnson Controls specialising in strategic benchmarking and outsourcing strategy reviews.

Stuart Mitchell is a Senior Engineer with the Commercial Business Unit of Johnson Controls specialising in maintenance strategy reviews and utilities management.

Professor Tim Morris is an Associate Professor at the London Business School, and researches and consults to a variety of professional service firms on strategic development and the management of change

John Berry is a Director of Ove Arup & Partners responsible for a multi-disciplinary design group of engineers. He has a particular interest in green issues and in strategic planning.

Acknowledgements

The NEW study, or more correctly, the New Environments for Working research project, was made possible by financial support from our Sponsors, all of whom also directly contributed to the progress of the study. Their interest was a great stimulus to the research effort. Their willingness to explore new ideas, to share their own experience, and to test novel hypotheses added greatly to the value of the research, in particular to its benefit for others in the design and manufacturing industries associated with the office workplace.

The study was generously supported by the Department of the Environment, Transport and the Region's Partners In Technology programme which provided not only 50% of the total research costs, but which also funded a series of seminars to discuss the findings with industry. These events assisted in the refinement of the conclusions of the study before its publication.

Particular thanks are due to:

Roger Berry	Department of the Environment, Transport and the Regions
John Sacks, Colin Watson	Arenson/President
Jonathan Emery	Hammerson
Peter Frackiewicz	Land Securities
Dr Danny Hann, Kevin Nix	National Power
Harvey Young	Johnson Controls
Edward McElhinney, Stuart Hodgkins	SAS Group
David King, Peter Atkinson	Interior
Bob Hargroves, Lou Bedocs	Thorn Lighting Group

The DEGW and BRE project team were also supported by several colleagues, and a small group of outside experts who contributed papers or presented at sponsors meetings. These included:

Anthony Slater and **Nigel Oseland** of BRE who provided information on lighting and comfort respectively.

RP Worden, whilst at Logica UK, who provided the paper which forms the basis of Chapter 21 - the future impact of software developments on the working environment.

Professor Tim Morris of the London Business School and **John Berry** of Ove Arup and Partners formed a small independent advisory group. They provided an in-depth understanding of organisational processes and behaviour, and a strategic technical approach to thinking on environmental systems for buildings, both of which proved to be highly beneficial in validating some of the methods used within the study.

Invaluable assistance was also provided by a group of organisations who agreed to be the subjects of case studies. Many individuals within these organisations helped with interviews, observations, and with the provision of plans and data, but special thanks are due to:

Richard H Korst	Andersen Consulting, Cleveland, Ohio, USA
David Hinton	Automobile Association, Thatcham, England
Marcia Witte	Change 2, England
A Katsman	Gasunie, Groningen, Netherlands
Reimar Unterlohner	Gruner & Jahr, Hamburg, Germany
Hugh Stebbing	Lloyds Bank, Bristol, England
Marcel Maassen	Rijksgebouwendienst, Haarlem, Netherlands
John Tenanes	Sun Microsystems, Menlo Park, California, USA
Art Kishiyama	Walt Disney Imagineering, Los Angeles, California,
Mick Dalton	Eastern Electricity, Ipswich
Siavash Mirnezami	Johnson Controls for IBM
Brian Forder	Royal Bank Of Scotland
Peter Yorke	University of East Anglia

Finally thanks are due to the New Environments for Working project team itself. The DEGW input was directed by **Dr Francis Duffy**, Chairman of DEGW, with the research effort co-ordinated by **Dr Andrew Laing**, Director of Research. **Denice Jaunzens** was responsible for coordinating the BRE research effort. A special mention must be made of **Steve Willis** who, when at BRE, initiated the proposal for the research and was involved in all of the early progress of ideas in the study. Also to **Jon Wilkins** who, when at BRE, was involved in the case study work and was especially important in contributing to the cost analysis part of the study.

Other members of DEGW and BRE who were involved in the three phases of the research project over its eighteen month life span, or have subsequently helped in the book production include:
From DEGW:
   Natalie Codling, Pamela Donleavy, Takumbo Howe, Ronen Journo, Nadia Kyriopoulou, Nicholas Morgan, David Tong

From BRE:
   Richard Fargus, Peter Grigg, David Warriner, Arron Perry, Ann Gibb, Ursula Garner.

Foreword

The nature of office work is changing, becoming less defined and predictable and much more fluid and fast changing. As a result office space and the environmental systems that serve it are having to become more flexible to cope with the diverse demands placed upon them as organisations move away from the regimented 9-5, one desk per staff member type of environment. The reasons for these changes are many and complex but include:

- The increasing pressures for businesses to become more customer focussed and therefore more dynamic and responsive to change;
- the opportunities offered by information and communications technologies that are reducing the importance of time and location to the modern business;
- social and demographic pressures as workers adapt to the need for flexibility but wish to establish an acceptable balance between work and home.

These changes have quite profound implications for our office buildings and workplaces. Businesses will no longer be tolerant of the need to adapt their activities to suit the buildings that are available, and increasingly they will challenge the high costs of refurbishment and churn. The market will place a premium on building and system designs that offer the maximum flexibility to adapt to the needs of changing business processes and patterns of use.

The New Environments for Working study is a welcome contribution to the growing debate on these issues. In particular it offers us:

- A language to describe working patterns in terms of their degrees of interaction and autonomy, and their use of space and time;
- a view of the ability of different building forms to adapt to the needs of differing patterns of work;
- a framework that will allow us to judge the ability of differing types of environmental systems to support differing patterns of work, and;
- guidance on the directions that designers and manufacturers should take as they seek to respond to increasingly dynamic client needs.

This book marks the culmination of a unique study which has brought together a powerful group of researchers, practitioners and manufacturers to look objectively at the implications of modern working practices for the specification and performance of building form and environmental systems. We believe that it offers a valuable framework within which all interested parties can debate the real issues faced by today's business organisations and bring forward improved designs for buildings, systems and products.

Martin Shaw
Research Director, BRE

Introduction

"Most office buildings and their environmental systems were designed for typical 9 to 5 activities, but how will they perform when that pattern of use changes?"

This question was the inspiration for the **New Environments for Working** (NEW) study. To answer it, we have defined a number of modern working patterns, and considered how a knowledge of these might influence the development of specifications for office construction and fit-out.

The four new metaphors devised to describe organisational patterns of work, and their spatial consequences, are *hive, den, cell* and *club.* Throughout this book, we describe how these concepts can be applied, and their consequences for office design and operation. This is examined from the perspective of the needs of office users, and of those responsible for procuring office space. We also consider trends in the application of these working patterns and the potential impact on product development.

This book examines what will be required from future office space, and how these client demands can be translated into a meaningful performance specification for the design team.

Part 1: Overview
In Part 1 we place the NEW study in context, describe its objectives, and summarise its findings. We begin by describing how changes in patterns of office use now demand a new approach to environmental services; ie HVAC (heating, ventilation and air-conditioning) and lighting. We then outline our research methods, summarising our main conclusions. These key findings are cross-referenced to detailed discussions in later chapters.

Part 2: A new research approach
In Part 2 we describe our research approach in greater detail, in particular how we developed models for the work patterns,

building types, and HVAC systems. We also consider the key influences on the life-cycle economics of a variety of office specification scenarios. Part 2 provides a common language which can help clients and their design teams (the demand and supply side of the procurement chain) to communicate more easily and effectively.

Part 3: Affinities between work patterns, building types, and environmental systems
In Part 3 we examine affinities between different combinations of building type, work pattern, and environmental system, using our findings to develop a number of rating tables which are likely to prove beneficial to:
- property professionals (by helping them assess the right client for the right building),
- suppliers (by helping them identify the target users for a product),
- designers (by suggesting starting points for their response to a client's brief),
- clients (by helping them specify and compare premises).

We also consider how changes in working patterns are likely to affect the specification of HVAC systems.(These findings can usefully be applied to all other fit-out elements).

Part 4: Case studies
In Part 4 we describe the practical case study work carried out to verify the usefulness of the model descriptions and affinity ratings. The brief summaries clearly illustrate the real implications of new ways of working and occupants' reactions to their workplace.

Part 5: Product directions and design implications
In Part 5 we consider likely future changes in the nature of office work. We highlight demands and opportunities for building and product developments, and consider how the role of information technology (IT) in the operation of the office will continue to increase in importance. This part of the book may be of particular interest to developers and suppliers of office products.

Bibliography and appendices

The appendices to this book contain a series of HVAC system definitions, further information on the questionnaires used in the study, and background information for the cost study.

Note

In this book, it is not our intention to recommend that you should choose a naturally ventilated or an air-conditioned design solution. This is a broader issue that is dealt with in several of the publications listed in the bibliography.

This book will be of special interest to:
- clients and their facilities managers
- designers, ie architects, space planners, engineers
- property professionals, ie developers, letting agents, portfolio managers
- suppliers, ie manufacturers of HVAC or lighting systems, and furniture.

Part 1: Overview

Part 1

Part 2

Part 3

Part 4

Part 5

Bibliography and
appendices

1 Objectives

This book contains the findings of **New Environments for Working**: a study of the implications of modern working practices for the specification and performance of building form and environmental systems. Our aim in this book is to present ideas for what could be done to improve the functionality of office buildings in the light of changing worker and organisational demands.

During the 1990s there have been many changes in the design and use of office buildings. Information Technology is introducing more irregular and intermittent working hours, and other practices that have transformed the daily use of the office. For some office workers the distinction between home and the workplace is no longer quite so clear as it used to be. They have become more demanding and their needs have become less predictable.

Most office design, especially of the lighting and ventilation systems, has been based upon grossly oversimplified notions of what goes on in the office. It has only recently become possible to measure easily where and when various office activities are actually carried out. These measurements show surprising findings regarding how often, and for what length of time, some work stations are left completely unattended.

No single office task now seems predominant: neither reading, telephone work, writing nor computer work. More time is typically spent away from the workplace. This is often in one-to-one meetings, and in activities which are highly interactive and mobile. As organisations begin to use IT to reorganise their use of office space and their working hours, new working patterns will become more common.

Most people regard office buildings and their environmental systems as more permanent entities than the organisational structures themselves. Despite the volatility of today's working patterns, however, office building design generally remains conservative. This situation cannot be allowed to last. Office buildings can inhibit organisational change, and once clients and users recognise this danger, they will insist on changes in the design of their buildings.

Our main objective in the **New Environments for Working** study was to explore these scenarios of probable change, and to determine the kinds of environmental and management systems in buildings that would satisfy these changing user demands.

In broader terms, we consider how environmental systems in office buildings need to relate to today's newer, more complex and more flexible working practices, organisational shape and performance. We believe that office environments must adapt to increasingly 'fluid' working practices (ie people whose working methods differ from 'traditional' practice; for example, operating to different hours and over a range of locations within the office building). This is increasingly matched, at both corporate and individual level, by an increasing demand for the reduction of energy waste and pollution – problems now associated with the over-servicing of office buildings.

In this study, we look at how environmental services can best respond to these emerging demands. We have synchronised the new forms of working with the new patterns of space and time use in the office, and the design of office buildings and office environmental services, by considering the following questions:

- What are the most effective and energy efficient ways of accommodating emerging working practices?
- What impact will these trends have on product development needs for HVAC systems?
- What implications will such trends have for the design of:
  - lighting systems?
  - the 'scenery', settings and furnishings of the office workplace?
  - the base building itself?

2 Methods of research

2.1 Four phases of research

The NEW study followed four phases of research. Phases 1–3 were carried out between October 1994 and March 1996. Phase 4 took place over the spring and summer of 1996.

Phase 1

During Phase 1, we created a number of models of office organisations representing the relationships between work patterns, use of space and buildings, and demands for environmental systems. Organisations were modelled as occupiers of typical kinds of buildings commonly found in the UK. A range of environmental systems was then evaluated against sets of performance requirements associated with these different patterns of work. A survey of leading services consultants was undertaken to evaluate the perceived effectiveness of a range of HVAC systems.

Phase 2

We carried out case studies of actual office organisations and contemporary office technologies to learn, from real examples, how the varied patterns of work are related to the use of space and their demand for environmental services. Following a widespread international literature search we identified eight organisations from the model of organisational behaviour developed in Phase 1. These were chosen to represent the full range of work patterns, rather than to illustrate any particular building type or environmental servicing technology.

The selection of the case studies was therefore driven by the priority of understanding the work process and the organisational 'demand' for space, technology, environmental servicing systems and buildings. As these organisations are based in the UK, Germany, Netherlands and the USA, they provide an interesting international cross-section of office accommodation and technical solutions.

A further four UK case studies focused on the performance of a range of innovative environmental systems and evaluated how well they could perform against the expected organisational demands.

Phase 3

Using the case studies and models from the first two phases, we developed a series of product directions and design implications for the re-design of environmental services, office buildings and interiors.

Johnson Controls (a project sponsor) developed a software-based model of the life-cycle cost profiles of different key combinations of organisational types and quality of fit-out solutions.

Finally, a consideration of the dynamics of these patterns of change in organisational structure led the project to specify strategic product directions or design implications for office buildings, HVAC and lighting systems, and the layout and furnishings of the workplace environment.

Phase 4

This final phase involved the controlled dissemination of the research findings. Over the spring and summer of 1996 a series of seminars were held with interested parties from industry — architects, interior designers, developers, letting agents, building services engineers, manufacturers, and facilities managers — to discuss and review a summary of the key findings. This feedback phase was again supported by the Department of the Environment, Transport and the Regions's Partners in Technology programme.

Background to the research programme

Our research approach draws on a long tradition of user-focused research at DEGW and BRE by concentrating on how people (collectively rather than as individual users) use space over time. We found that we were best able to understand users' demands and requirements by focusing on the social reality of the groups and organisations of which they form an active part. Individual office users are regarded in representative groups: as members of socially interacting institutions which have identifiable directions, motivations, and interests. In this way, we have defined the richer image of the complex, collective entity of the corporate organisation.

Before we could begin to design the office environment for such user groups, our first task had to be to understand and evaluate their needs. The starting point was the recognition that organisations are driven to respond to an increasingly turbulent business environment. They must respond to the competitive market, often undergoing rapid change and even conflict, as part of their way of handling economic survival and the support of their most vital resource: their own human capital.

Designers must somehow take into account this complex and dynamic picture. This can only be achieved successfully through a rigorous understanding of how an organisation's business process can be translated into requirements for environmental and spatial solutions that are based clearly on defined patterns of use over time.

The research problem is therefore how to understand and model the relationships between the social structure and technology of office organisations. From this we can move to look at how the quality and nature of the spatial environment can be maintained throughout any changes in these relationships.

DEGW has for many years specialised in the systematic modelling of user requirements and in using these models to evaluate the performance of buildings. The method has always been typological. In the 1980s, DEGW and others undertook the pioneering ORBIT (Organisational Research, Buildings and Information Technology) studies which plotted the impact of IT on the nature of the office work process, and on the design of the office building. Following this, building appraisal techniques were developed for measuring, benchmarking and planning the new wave of large offices being built in the City of London. One example of this is the planning of the building types used in the landmark Broadgate development in the City of London.

In the 1990s this approach was developed through two major projects. 'The Responsible Workplace' study (coordinated jointly by DEGW and BRE) investigated the new concerns of office users and highlighted demands for office buildings that would add value to organisational performance, whilst minimising occupancy costs and environmental impacts (Duffy, Laing and Crisp, 1993).

Simultaneously DEGW and Teknibank completed the 'Intelligent Building in Europe' study that established a new way of conceptualising building intelligence focused on user needs, rather than on the conventional technical evaluation of building performance. This developed a number of building appraisal methods that contributed to an intelligent building rating system. The appraisal methods have been further evolved and refined in work for the 'Intelligent Building in South East Asia' study completed in 1995. A further Intelligent Building study is now being carried out in Latin America.

Underlying all this research into organisations and buildings has been a simple premise that it is possible to model user requirements and translate them into design and performance criteria for buildings, provided that the patterns of time and space use are fully understood.

In the NEW study this tradition of typological understanding of user requirements and building design has been deepened and extended. For the first time this theoretical approach has included user demands for environmental services in relation to different work patterns and building types.

3 Conclusions

This chapter summarises the findings of the NEW study, under the following headings:
- Work patterns and building types
- Environmental systems and user demands
- Case studies
- Cost implications
- Affinities between work patterns, building types and environmental systems
- Dynamics of change
- Product directions and design implications.

Work patterns and building types

From modelling emerging work patterns and testing typical office building configurations against them (chapters 5 and 6) we conclude:

- Not all office organisations make the same arrangements regarding office space and working hours. Any organisation will have its own expectations of what the environmental systems within its premises should offer.

- We have created four fundamental group-types (or models) called *hive, cell, den,* and *club* (see page 9). Each group has its own requirements for space use and environmental services. Most organisations, and parts of organisations, are composed of more than one work pattern. To identify these groups, we used two 'key' variables. These were:

  - the 'degrees of interaction'; ie how much did office workers need to work or communicate face-to-face with their colleagues?
  - the 'degrees of individual autonomy'; ie how much control does any employee have over the hours he or she works, the work location, the nature of the work, and the tools provided to do that work?

Using our four organisational models we can map the current location of an organisation. We can also observe the dynamics of change, ie broader trends in the patterns of work being exhibited. For example, we expect the largest movement will be away from the *hive* and *cell* towards the *den* and *club* models.

- Over the next ten years, many organisations will become more interactive and more intermittent in their patterns of occupation of office space. Many will experiment with space use intensification. These are characteristics of the *club* model.

Significance of the findings
The significance of the conclusions of the NEW study is best illustrated by comparing them with the recommendations of such compilations of advanced office design practice as the British Council for Offices' (BCO) specification. The BCO, drawing on the experience of leading developers, designers and surveyors in the late eighties and early nineties, makes a number of very pertinent recommendations for office designers wishing to avoid over specification, yet provide a robust and desirable building. They:
- react against the tendency, common in late eighties office developments, to over-specify in such matters as cooling loads;
- are environmentally aware and sensitive in common with such standards as BREEAM;
- acknowledge the potential of innovative environmental systems to reconcile users' preferences for natural ventilation with the need to accommodate increasing amounts of electronic equipment.

What the BCO specification, from the perspective of the NEW Study, does not adequately do is to recognise that:
- office organisations are inherently diverse and are likely to become more so;
- assumptions of consistent patterns of occupancy over the working day or the working week are increasingly unrealistic;
- users will not only increasingly resist hermetically sealed environments, but will want more and more control over their own comfort, not just as individuals but also as members of teams and groups;
- central control of environmental systems is likely to be increasingly challenged.

- Practically, within this ten year period, what will be more important for office designers than any 'ideal' model of the eventual *club* destination, will be the migration from the traditional *hive* office model to more interactive and more intermittent patterns of occupancy as much *hive* work will either be automated or exported to low-wage economies.
- The building forms that can best accommodate these migrations, as well as the ultimate *club* destination, are the *atrium* and *medium depth* buildings. *Deep central core* and *shallow depth* configurations are less adaptive and hence comparatively vulnerable to change.

Environmental systems and user demands

From testing which families of HVAC systems offer the most potential for accommodating emerging patterns of user occupancy associated with new ways of working (chapter 7) we conclude that:

- The four families of HVAC systems we have defined in the NEW study meet the current needs of users in different ways.
- Existing environmental systems meet the relatively simple requirements of the *hive* and the *cell* office more easily than those of the more complex patterns of the *den* and *club*.
- To satisfy emerging demands for the *den* and *club*, environmental systems will have to be designed to be considerably more adaptive to change and responsive to user needs.
- The three-sided relationship of (1) work pattern to HVAC system; (2) HVAC system to building type; and (3) work pattern to building type, complicates any general discussion of which HVAC systems are likely to be most requested in the future. *Distributed* systems score well under a large proportion of the *den* or *club* scenarios with different building type. A *mixed mode* system (that is a strategic combination of natural and mechanical ventilation solutions) also appears to offer benefits over a wide range of building forms.

Case studies

From a series of case studies chosen to illustrate a range of environmental systems in use by a cross-section of organisational types (chapters 14–16), we conclude that:

- The case study findings support the existence of work patterns that use space, environmental systems, and building types in different ways. This lends credence to the approach of developing models and their associated demands adopted by the NEW study.

Some organisations have successfully introduced innovations in how they organise working practices, working hours, and the use of space, despite having to work with unsuitable buildings and environmental systems. Others have relocated, often at great expense, to buildings with environmental systems which, in some respects, were highly over-designed.

Before evaluating environmental systems the following factors must be considered:

- how well are they integrated in the buildings that contain them?
- how well do they perform over a period of time?
- how cost effective are they on a life-cycle basis?

Cost implications

From modelling the costs of key combinations of working patterns, building forms and fit-out elements of different qualities (Chapter 8), we conclude that:

- Some building types and some environmental systems result in inherently higher costs in use.
- The more advanced organisational types (*den* and *club*) tend to make heavier demands on environmental systems than the *hive*, but demand less than the *cell*. The costs of environmental systems for these organisational types are therefore likely to reflect these demands.
- Such higher costs in use can be ameliorated by not attempting to accommodate such organisations in the *deep central core* building type which is inherently expensive to run. Whilst the *atrium* building type is also expensive to run these buildings offer enhanced adaptability to accommodate the migration towards more advanced organisational types.

The hive, cell, den and club models

Den
We believe this model will become increasingly important as team processes become more common in the office. The *den* is associated with group work. The *den* worker is interactive but not necessarily highly autonomous, carrying out tasks that are typically of short duration and team-based.

The space is designed for group working, with a range of simple settings in the open plan or group room that encourage interaction. There is also access to some shared facilities.

Typical den organisations
Design, insurance, media and advertising.

Club
This model is likely to become increasingly common as IT and organisational theory develop. It challenges the simplistic assumptions upon which most North American and North European office design is based. The *club* is for knowledge work: both autonomous and interactive. The pattern of occupancy is intermittent and over an extended working day. A wide variety of shared task based settings serve both concentrated individual and group interactive work.

Individuals and teams occupy space on an as-needed basis, moving around the space to take advantage of a wide range of facilities.

Typical club organisations
Advertising or management consultancies, IT companies, and other high-value-adding knowledge workers in many sectors.

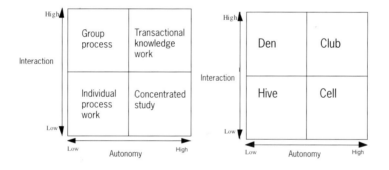

Hive
This model describes the vast majority of office buildings and office environmental systems. The *hive* is associated with individual process work, little interaction and low levels of individual autonomy.

Staff sit at simple workstations for continuous periods of time on a regular schedule.
The settings are typically uniform, open planned, screened and impersonal.

Typical hive organisations
Telesales, call centres, routine banking, financial, and administrative operations and information services.

Cell
This is the model upon which many Northern European offices have been designed since the 1980s. The *cell* is for individuals involved in concentrated work with little interaction. Highly autonomous individuals occupy the office in an intermittent and irregular pattern with extended working hours. They spend many hours working away from the office.

Each individual uses either an enclosed *cell* or a highly screened workstation for a wide variety of tasks. This working space may be shared.

Typical cell organisations
Law, some parts of accountancy, academic offices and some research and consultancy organisations.

- Occupancy costs per head (rather than per square metre) can be greatly reduced by using 'advanced' working practices which intensify the use of space (eg by sharing workstations and other settings). However, as this can be applied to a number of organisational types, it should not be the deciding factor for specifying environmental systems that turn out to be costly to run or use.

Affinities between work patterns, building types and environmental systems

As part of our research into the demands for environmental services we identified a number of profiles associated with different patterns of work and with different patterns of space use. By using these profiles, we were able to see the relationships between patterns of work, building types, and environmental services as a set of 'affinities'.

By 'affinity' we mean the relationship of the supplied building type or environmental system to the demands of the specific work pattern. This relationship can be viewed as a 'match' or as a degree of appropriateness. We plotted our theoretical degrees of affinity between patterns of work, building types, and environmental systems and gave them relative values (poor, adequate, or good). We then justified these values by explanations derived from the research model and from the case studies.

These values can never be prescriptive. Many excellent buildings have been, and will be designed, which may contradict these evaluations. Nevertheless, the concept of affinities gives us an opportunity to explore more precisely the ways in which the emerging demands of new ways of working are likely to impact on the requirements for systems and buildings. It also forms a starting point for a dialogue between the client and the design team.

From examining, first separately and then in an integrated way, the series of relationships between building types and organisational types, between environmental systems and organisational types, and between building types and environmental systems (Chapters 9–11), we conclude that:
- The requirements of the most advanced organisations (the *club*) are likely to be more readily satisfied with *mixed mode* and *distributed* HVAC systems. These systems are relatively easily accommodated in all

four major office building types (*shallow plan, medium depth, deep plan*, and *atrium*) as used in ECON19, published by BRECSU (Building Research Energy Conservation Support Unit) at BRE.
- The requirements of the simplest types of organisation (the *hive*) are best met either by conventional *all air* or the more innovative *radiative air* systems.
- The *cell* is the most difficult working pattern to accommodate in terms of building form, being only highly compatible with one building type: the *medium depth* slab office.
- The key issue for the *den* organisation is how to enable group consensus based decisions. This is best served by *all air* or *distributed* systems in the *medium depth* or *atrium* building types.

Dynamics of change

From reviewing likely trends in organisational development (Chapter 13), and after considering the transition that many organisations are likely to make (particularly from *hive* and *cell* to *den* and *club*), we conclude that:
- The main longer term trend in organisations is towards becoming more interactive and more intermittent in the use of time and space by individuals and groups.
- Most larger organisations will continue to consist of a mix of the four organisational types: it is the proportion of each that will shift over time.
- The office building types that have the most capacity for accommodating this shift in organisational demand are the *atrium*, and *medium depth* slabs.
- The most appropriate environmental systems to facilitate this shift in organisational demand are likely to be more responsive and controllable at a local level than conventional *radiative* or *all air* types.

Product directions and design implications

The following recommendations on product development and design are based on the main conclusions of the NEW study (Chapters 17–20).

Recommendations for individual users
- Environmental systems should provide a higher degree of control, both for individuals and groups, than is available at present.
- Environmental systems should be much more accessible and simpler for users to operate than at present.
- Environmental systems and their controls should be designed with more sensitivity to

users' needs. This should facilitate the transition from continuous work patterns that are low in interaction to patterns of work which are certain to be quite the opposite.

- There should be a sharper distinction between the level of environment provided for 'people spaces' - which will tend to be for highly mobile and changing groups - and for the zones provided for support activities.
- Environmental systems should be able to cope with adapting ratios between people and support zones, since the latter will tend to increase in many office organisations.

Recommendations for clients
- Clients need guidance on how to avoid investing in, and commissioning or leasing, buildings which are designed too specifically for one work pattern.

Recommendations for developers
- Produce simple, straightforward *medium depth* and *atrium* office shells. Avoid *shallow* and *deep* plan types unless they are for specific purposes, or to meet the needs of the client.
- Ensure the simplest possible interfaces by using high degrees of detachment between environmental systems and building shells, ie the ability to decouple services from fabric to allow for flexibility and adaptability.
- Allow enough space and volume to permit adaptation to existing services and to facilitate the provision of additional services in zones identified for support activities, ie a contingency or a zoned *mixed mode* approach (for definitions of *mixed mode* approaches see Chapter 10).
- Anticipate shorter leases and multi-tenancy. Invent ways of providing shared common services for building occupants on a commercial basis.

Recommendations for HVAC services manufacturers
- Provide controls which can respond quickly and cost-effectively to changing patterns of occupancy, without adversely affecting the quality of the environment.
- Provide intelligent controls for individuals, teams and support spaces that allow maximum discretion for users and minimise operating costs. Greatly simplify the user interface.
- Develop strategies for effective *mixed mode* operations. Focus on *distributed* systems because user demand for them is more likely to increase most quickly.

- Consider how *radiative* and *all air* systems might be improved to operate more effectively within a *mixed mode* strategy.
- Re-think the design of conventional *radiative* and *all air* systems to include the finer forms of control and responsiveness required by *den* and *club* organisations.
- Enhance the effectiveness of maintenance routines through advanced monitoring and control techniques, and developing systems which are inherently easier to maintain.

Recommendations for lighting designers and manufacturers
- Consider the demands for lighting products raised by different work patterns.
- Develop lighting to support 24-hour shift working (*hive*).
- Respond to new forms of video communication and IT use.
- Allow individuals and teams to control lighting, especially in areas used for meetings, training and other communal activities.
- Improve the design of lighting controllers so that they are more intelligent and responsive to the needs of the individual. Consider standardisation to enable ease of use.
- Design more multi-task adjustable task lighting to suit shared settings used by different individuals (*club*).
- Anticipate more finely tuned occupancy sensing for lighting *den*, *cell*, and *club* environments. (These work patterns are typified by a wide range of tasks, carried out by a fluctuating number of occupants.)
- Improve the integration of lighting strategy with HVAC approaches in base building design. Consider the implications of a trend towards exposed thermal mass in ceilings.

Recommendations for furniture manufacturers
- Focus on specifying furniture products that support interactive, intermittent work processes. In this way you will become less reliant on supplying products for one-to-one desk occupancy.
- Provide furniture adapted to more zoning of work requirements: quiet areas, meetings spaces, customer interface etc.
- Develop furniture systems which can enhance individual and team control of the working environment.
- Improve the interface between organisations, buildings, and environmental systems by improving the design of partitions, ceilings and access floors.

Part 2: A new research approach

Part 1

Part 2

Part 3

Part 4

Part 5

Bibliography and
appendices

4 The research model

Affinities between the work patterns, the building types and the environmental systems

4.1 The research agenda

The ways of working in offices are changing radically, new ways of working across time and space are emerging. Organisations are eager to re-examine the means by which they can add value to their performance by re-engineering their approach to the use of buildings, space and facilities. A model of organisations' demands for environmental services is developed from examining how these kinds of changing patterns of work affect the building and its internal environment.

New ways of working are argued to be both more highly interactive and to provide individuals with greater autonomy over the timing, content, tools and locations of work. The content of work is more varied and creative, work is undertaken in ways that are more mobile and nomadic than conventional office work. The design of office buildings and their environmental systems may inhibit these more dynamic ways of using space and time. Most office buildings, interiors and environmental systems are briefed, designed, built, serviced and occupied without regard to these emerging organisational demands.

The new ways of working in offices are eroding the idea of nine-to-five office hours. Even today the time of working is erratic and often extended, sometimes even linked to global 'follow-the-sun' activities. The impact on space is difficult to predict, often resulting in uneven patterns of high density space use. Density itself, the numbers of people occupying space, has to be measured in new ways as innovative ways of working are often accommodated in ways that intensify the use of space over time.

Not only is the pattern of space occupancy over time extended and intensified, but the very notion of office space and office design is challenged and transformed. Taking the place of the one-person-to-an-office-or-desk

stereotype, an assumption that has driven office design and planning for a century, is the idea of the office as a series of spaces designed to support a wide range of different tasks and activities.

These task-based settings are only used on an as-needed basis. They form part of a spectrum of places where work occurs, other locations include the home, the client's premises and other 'third places' such as airports, stations, cars, and on the street.

Another way of putting this is to recognise the implicit assumptions of conventional office design that fail to match the expectations of organisations working in new ways. The conventional office workplace assumes wrongly that:
- office work is routine and undertaken largely by individuals working alone;
- staff work regular 9 to 5 days;
- everyone has their 'own' desk or office at which they sit all day;
- most people are in the building during the course of the day and week;
- the range of space standards and settings for office is work is simple and hierarchical;
- information technology is fixed to desks and does not move around.

The problem with office design, and with the suppliers of office products, is that both have looked to the past. Organisations who are working in new, unconventional, quite different ways, are ahead of designers and suppliers in their thinking about the nature of the office.

They are developing different and higher expectations for:
- their control of time and place;
- where they work;
- the quality of the work environment;
- the healthiness of their workplace and their lifestyles.

This is because office organisations have changed how they work:

From	To
routine processes	creative knowledge work
individual tasks	groups, teams, and projects
alone	interactive.

They have changed where they work:

From	To
places	networks
central	dispersed
transport	communication
office	multiple locations including the home.

They are changing their use of information technologies:

From	To
data	knowledge
central	distributed
mainframe	PC, video, telecomms, e-mail, Internet
one place	mobile, personal, nomadic, virtual
big	palmtop, pocket, laptop.

They are using space over time in new ways:

From	To
one desk per person	shared group and individual settings
hierarchical space standards	diverse task based space
9 to 5 at one place	anywhere, anytime
under-occupancy	varied patterns of high density use
owned	shared.

4.2 A model of demand and supply

The implications of these new ways of working for the design of the office and its environmental systems are explored through the analysis of the relationship between the work process and the patterns of space use. This results in the identification of four part organisational, part spatial, types: *hive, cell, den* and *club*.

The logic of development of these types is explored in the following section, it forms the basis of the demand side of the modelling exercise. Each organisational/spatial type modelled represents significant differences in terms of:
● patterns of work
● patterns of occupancy of space over time
● patterns of use of information technology
● type of space layout and furniture systems
● type of demand for environmental services
● affinity with different building types.

A variety of types of space designs (and space ownership and management systems) and expected demands for environmental services can be conceptualised in relation to fundamental differences identified in patterns of work. Characteristic space layouts and work settings that correspond to these ways of working and patterns of use of space over time are developed and illustrated. These represent what we have termed the 'demand' profiles of the organisation.

These 'demands' of organisations are then analysed against the constraints and opportunities of the 'supply' of building types, for which a separate typology is developed. This permits informed judgements to be made about how well the 'demands' are met by the 'supply'. The result of the modelling exercise is a picture of the directions of expected demands made by various types of organisations, particularly those working in new ways; of how these patterns of demand affect the quality and degrees of control of environmental systems; and how these demands can be met by different generic building types and environmental systems.

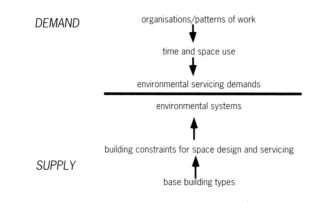

DEMAND   organisations/patterns of work

↓

time and space use

↓

environmental servicing demands

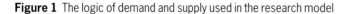

environmental systems

↑

building constraints for space design and servicing

SUPPLY

↑

base building types

Figure 1 The logic of demand and supply used in the research model

This pattern of demand of the organisation therefore cascades through several levels of impacts: from the pattern of work, through the pattern of time and space use, to the nature of the demand for environmental services. The demand is then contained within, and affected by, the constraints and opportunities offered by: the hierarchy of building supply elements; the base building shell and its configuration; the limitations of space design and associated environmental servicing affinities; and the scope and performance attributes of the environmental systems themselves. The logic of the research model derived from understanding these interactions of organisational demand and building supply is shown in Figure 1.

This model of organisational demand and building supply, within which environmental services are prescribed, must also be related to the dynamic pattern of the life-cycle of the

elements of the building and its components. The typical life-cycle of elements of generic office buildings has been described by DEGW in previous studies (DEGW and others. *ORBIT 1.* 1985), see Figure 2.

These life-cycle elements represent components of the 'supply' of buildings, of which environmental services are a significant part. An important feature of the hierarchy of life-cycle elements is that the shorter life-cycle elements are much more amenable to user control and change. They therefore bear a more immediate relationship to the different demands made by the types of organisations modelled here.

It is most significant that the environmental servicing element of this hierarchy is positioned midway between the most 'supply' dominated feature of the building (the long-term building shell) and the most 'demand' oriented features of the hierarchy of life-cycle elements (the settings of the office which may be changed daily or hourly by the end users).

In this sense, 'environmental services' are mediated strongly in relationships at both the demand and supply levels of the interface between the organisation (the end users) and the built and designed environment. Thus, in many respects it is environmental services that bridge between the building 'supply' and the user 'demand'. The linkages between environmental services and all of the levels of the supply of the building, from the shell to the everyday settings of the office, are extensive.

1 Shell
50–75 years
(structure, cladding)

2 Services
15 years
(heat, ventilation, light, power)

3 Scenery
5 years
(fixed interior elements: ceiling, partitions, finishes, IT equipment)

4 Settings
Day to day rearrangement of office furnishing

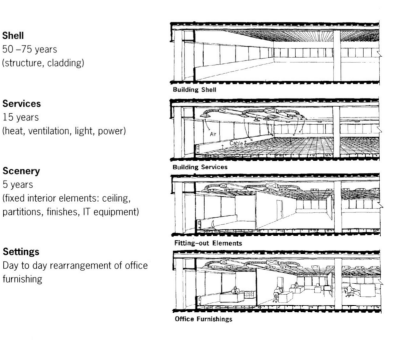

Figure 2 The life-cycle elements of typical office buildings

This suggests that the attempts to optimise the quality of servicing in response to changing organisational demands and ways of working will have impacts at every level of the design, management and use of the building supply.

Leaman and Bordass (in *The Responsible Workplace;* Duffy, Laing and Crisp, 1993) have explored these issues of the hierarchy of control in buildings in more detail. Leaman and Borden argue that the hierarchy of building shell, services, settings and tasks should be better managed and designed so that the degree of constraints imposed by one level upon the others is minimised; and that vertical feedback and monitoring between and across the levels of the hierarchy should be optimised: "a science of decision making will develop around the total building system" (*The Responsible Workplace*; Duffy, Laing and Crisp, 1993, p. 32).

The modelling exercise of the NEW study is concerned to understand the relationships between three core sets of variables in this hierarchy of building and user relationships: the work patterns, the HVAC systems, and the building types. Within each of these core sets of variables we have identified four generic types in order to explore the complex relationships identified.

Environmental systems are normally taken to include both HVAC and lighting systems. However in this study the majority of the analysis has been directed towards HVAC systems as the number of options is large, well defined, and the selection process more complex.

The modelling of each of these sets of generic types is explored in the following sections.

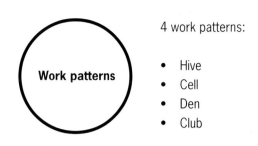

4 work patterns:

- Hive
- Cell
- Den
- Club

Figure 4 Four work patterns

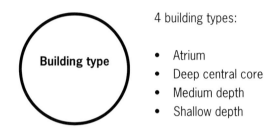

4 building types:

- Atrium
- Deep central core
- Medium depth
- Shallow depth

Figure 5 Four building types

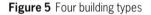

4 HVAC system families

- Distributed systems
- All-air systems
- Radiative/air systems
- Mixed mode systems

Figure 6 Four HVAC system types

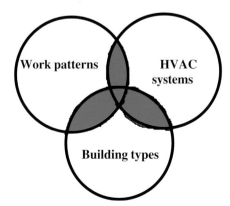

Figure 3 Modelling three sets of relationships

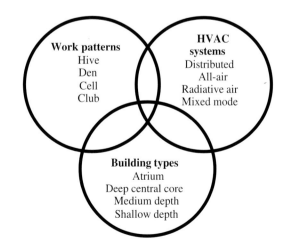

Figure 7 Relationships between work patterns, HVAC systems and building types

5   The work pattern model

5.1 Patterns of work and the use of space over time

Changes in the patterns of work are associated with an increasing complexity in the variety of work settings and spatial layouts. Organisations working in new ways are able to instigate new patterns of space ownership and management: they share space over time in the office and thereby increase the effective density of the occupancy of the space they use. Some of the key differences between conventional and new ways of working are summarised in Figure 8 and highlighted in Figure 9.

	Conventional	New
Pattern of work	routine	creative
	individual tasks	group, project, team
	isolated	interactive
Occupancy	9 to 5	extended
	own desk/office	shared as-needed
	low utilisation	high utilisation
	low density	high density
Settings	status based	task based
	single setting	multiple/varied settings
	multi-purpose	zoned

Figure 8 Summary of differences in work patterns and space occupancy

In exploring the implications of new ways of working for the design of the office, the project team concentrated on the relationships between the patterns of the work process and the use of space. The central issues are the degrees to which the mode of working of the organisation (or of the group within the organisation) is **interactive** or **autonomous**. These two variables are critical to understanding the impact of patterns of work, especially new ways of working, on the use and design of the office workplace and on its associated environmental servicing.

By **interaction** we mean the degree of personal face-to-face interaction, primarily within the individual's working group, as being significant in terms of its impacts on environmental and spatial demands. The forms of interaction are very varied, ranging formal and informal through meetings and other ad hoc encounters. Interactions via the computer, telephone, or other virtual media are not as significant in this regard, but need consideration in so far as they supplement or substitute for face-to-face interaction both now and in the future. Other forms of interaction, with other units and with other groups or individuals outside the organisation, are also relevant in so far as they will have an impact on the pattern of occupancy of space. Many external face-to-face interactions imply a more intermittent pattern of space occupancy.

By **autonomy** we mean the degree of control, responsibility and discretion the individual has over the content, method, location, and tools of the work process.

The degrees of interaction and autonomy will furthermore be associated with the degrees to which the pattern of space use is likely to be continuous or intermittent. Higher degrees of interaction and individual autonomy are often associated with more intermittent patterns of space occupancy. Individuals with greater discretion over the timing, content and tools of work will be more likely to want or need to work in several different locations both within and outside the office. They may choose to work at home some of the time or may spend time at their clients' premises.

Individuals whose work is highly interactive will spend more time away from their 'own' desks because they need to meet or work with others either inside or outside the office workplace. They are thereby also potentially associated with a greater capacity for sharing of space over time or 'space use intensification'.

Conventional and new ways of working: key assumptions

	Conventional office assumptions	New ways of working
Patterns of work	Routine processes Individual tasks Isolated work	Creative knowledge work Groups, teams, projects Interactive work
Patterns of occupancy of space over time	Central office locations in which staff are assumed to occupy individual workstations on a full-time basis, typically over the course of the 9 to 5 day. The office assumes one desk per person; provides a hierarchy of space standards (whether open planned or enclosed); and is occupied typically at levels at least 30% below full capacity. Work settings are individually 'owned'.	The 'office' is replaced by a distributed set of work locations linked by networks of communication in which highly autonomous individuals work in project teams and groups. The nature of work is nomadic and mobile occurring in a wide variety of work settings inside and outside the office building, including the home. The daily timetable is extended and irregular. Work settings are not 'owned' by individuals but are occupied on an as-needed basis and provided to serve a variety of tasks, both individual and group. The sharing of space enables the daily occupancy of space to be at or near capacity.
Type of space layout, furniture systems and use of space and buildings	Rigid hierarchy of space standards and furniture related to status and rank rule the space layout, whether open or enclosed. The individual allocation of space predominates over group or interactive meeting spaces.	Multiple shared group work and individual task based settings. The settings, layout and furniture of the office are geared to the work process and its tasks.
Use of information technology	Information technology often used for routine data processing, terminals in fixed positions served by mainframes.	Technology used to support creative knowledge work, both individual and group. File servers support a variety of IT tools, including PCs and laptops, and shared specialised equipment. Focus on mobility and on IT equipment to be used in a wide variety of settings. An environment of communication with video and audio conferencing and the use of images in a variety of ways.

Figure 9 Conventional and new ways of working: key assumptions

Thus, degrees of interaction and autonomy correlate strongly with many aspects of the design, servicing and control of the environment. They affect expectations for:

● openness or enclosure of the space;
● heights of partitions, screens, walls, or other space dividing elements;
● forms of control over environmental services and lighting, whether group or individual, whether highly controllable or not;
● zoning, individual ownership.

Characteristic space layouts and work settings that correspond with these ways of working and patterns of use of space over time are developed and illustrated later in this chapter. The detailed design of these various environments will depend on other factors, particularly:

● the duration of the pattern of the use of space over time;
● the variety of the content of work tasks.

Depending on the degree to which the organisation (or part of it) is expected to work in these different ways, then a variety of types of space layouts, and associated ownership and management systems are modelled. The expected demands for environmental services and systems associated with these work patterns and space types are also modelled.

A series of diagrams illustrates these over-lapping characteristics and the affinities between work pattern, space design and occupancy, and the demands for

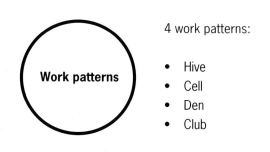

Figure 10 Four work patterns

environmental services. They offer a way of thinking through the impact of new ways of working on the design of the office environment. They are not intended to provide in themselves the detailed design solutions for particular organisations.

Four major organisational types are identified with distinct work patterns and associated spatial design features using the above approach. They represent a range of both conventional and new ways of working. They are a shorthand description of a set of affinities between the work pattern, the use of space, and the demands likely to be made by these organisations or working groups for space and environmental services. The organisational/spatial types are called: *hive, cell, den* and *club*.

The following sections describe these work patterns, how they would be expected to use space, and show some typical examples of organisations of these kinds.

The hive

The *hive* office organisation is characterised by individual routine process work with low levels of interaction and individual autonomy. The office worker sits at simple workstations for continuous periods of time on a regular 9 to 5 schedule (variants of this type include 24-hour shift working). The settings are typically uniform, open planned, screened and impersonal. Typical organisations or work groups include telesales, call centres, data entry or processing, routine banking, financial and administrative operations, and basic information services.

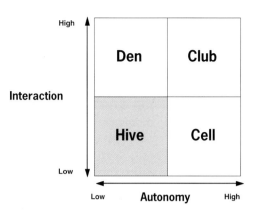

Figure 11 The *hive* work pattern: low interaction, low autonomy

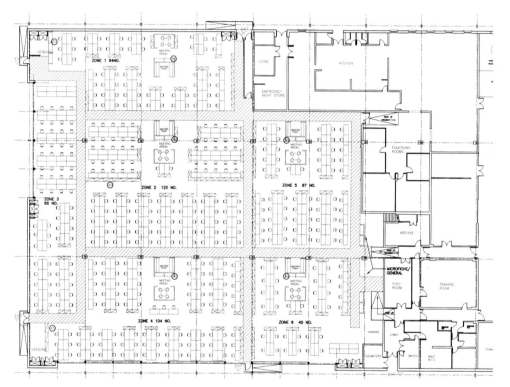

Figure 12 Plan of British Gas offices at Barnet, England. Source: DEGW (Architects: DEGW)

Figure 13 Interior of British Gas offices at Barnet, England. Source: DEGW (Architects: DEGW)

The cell

The *cell* office organisation is for individual concentrated work with little interaction. Highly autonomous individuals occupy the office in an intermittent irregular pattern with extended working days, working elsewhere some of the time (possibly at home, at clients, or on the road).

Each individual is typically provided with the use of either an enclosed cell or a highly screened workstation in an open planned office. Each individual setting must provide for a complex variety of tasks. The autonomous pattern of work, implying a sporadic and irregular occupancy of the space means that the potential exists for the settings needed by the individual to be planned and used on a shared basis. Typical organisations include lawyers, some accountancy firms, academic offices, research organisations and management consultancies.

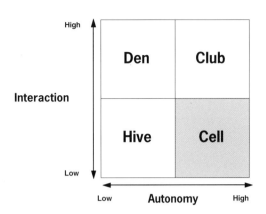

Figure 14 The cell work pattern: low interaction, high autonomy

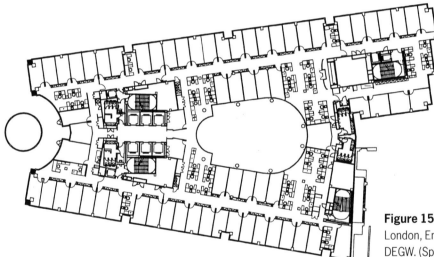

Figure 15 Plan of Freshfields, London, England. Source: DEGW. (Space planning and interior design by DEGW)

Figure 16 Interior of Freshfields, London, England. Source: DEGW (Space planning and interior design by DEGW)

The den

The *den* office organisation is associated with group process work, interactive but not necessarily highly autonomous. The space is designed for group working with a range of several simple settings, typically arranged in the open plan or group room. While the settings are normally designed on the assumption that every individual occupies their 'own' desk, the group would also have access to local ancillary space for shared equipment or special technical facilities that are used as-needed. Tasks are typically of short duration involving team work. Typical organisations include design, research, some media work and advertising.

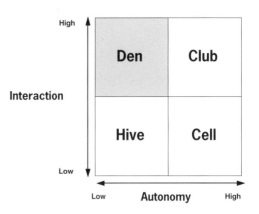

Figure 17 The *den* work pattern, high interaction, low autonomy

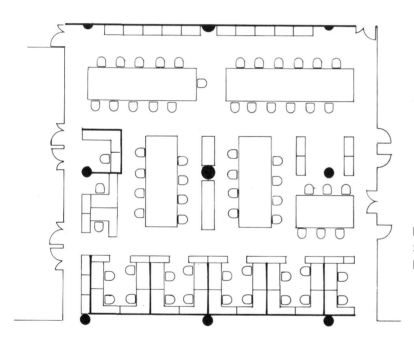

Figure 18 Plan of ITN headquarters, Source: DEGW. (Architects: Sir Norman Foster & Partners)

Figure 19 Interior of ITN headquarters, Source: DEGW (Architects: Sir Norman Foster & Partners)

The club

The *club* office organisation is for knowledge work: both highly autonomous and highly interactive. The pattern of occupancy is intermittent and over an extended working day. A wide variety of shared task based settings serve both concentrated individual and group interactive work. Individuals and teams occupy space on an as-needed basis, moving around the space to take advantage of a wide range of facilities.

The ratio of sharing will depend on the precise content of the work activity and the mix of in-house versus out-of-office working, possibly combining tele-working, home-working and working at client and other locations. Typical organisations include some creative firms such as advertising and media companies,

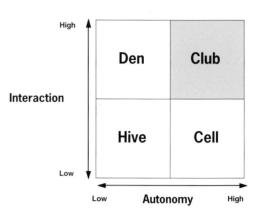

Figure 20 The *club* work pattern, high interaction, high autonomy

IT companies, and some management consultancies and the general category of high value-adding knowledge workers in many sectors.

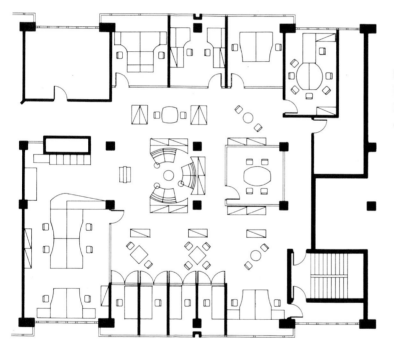

Figure 21 Plan of Rijksgebouwendienst, Haarlem, Netherlands. Source: DEGW. (Interior design by Gispen)

Figure 22 Interior of Rijksgebouwendienst, Haarlem, Netherlands. Source: DEGW

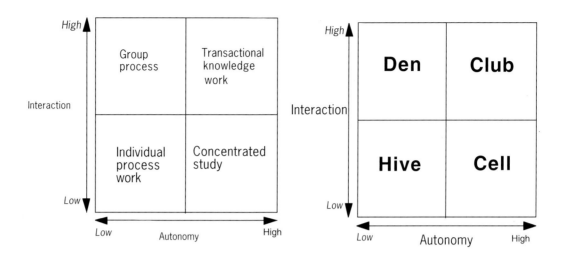

Figure 23 Patterns of work: four major types

The work pattern characteristics of the four organisational types are summarised in Figure 23.

The limits of this typology of organisations should be recognised. First, the terms *hive*, *cell*, *den* and *club* may usefully be applied at different scales or to separate parts of the organisation. Organisations differ very widely in the degree of internal variety of work processes and patterns. Parts of organisations with different work patterns may be located in separate buildings or parts of floors. The specific correlation between work pattern and space occupancy will vary widely.

It is recognised that most organisations, or parts of some organisations, will no doubt be represented by combinations of these work patterns. For example, many organisations have 'back office' groups of staff engaged in data entry or routine administrative functions, which we have referred to as *hive*, which may be located with other groups operating as a *den* or a *club* in an headquarters office building.

A dynamic way of using the model is to identify the relative proportions of organisational types within the one organisation or location, and then to think through the implications of future organisational change on their relative importance. The correlations between this combination of 'types' and their implications for buildings, space use, environmental servicing, can all be articulated. The use of the model in this dynamic way is summarised in Chapter 13.

It should also be noted that the above typology does not preclude any one sector or type of work from being included in any one of the types. We believe the diversity of organisations is such that even within the same sector of work or profession sufficient differences in work style and organisational structure may exist to preclude any inevitable association between particular sectors and the individual types defined here. On the other hand, we do expect to see affinities between some sectors of work and the typologies outlined. Such an affinity exists, for example, between many of the large IT firms, other creative organisations, as well as some of the management consultancy firms and the *club* type offices.

6   The building type model

6.1 Types of space layout and patterns of use

For each of the four patterns of work, the project team developed hypothetical space plan layouts over the typical floors of each of four typical building types (see below). A set of assumptions was created to define how the space would be used over time in each organisation, including the degrees to which space would be shared over time. The core assumptions used in the modelling exercise are described in Figure 27.

A database was created in which all the types of spaces, the distribution of information technology equipment, and patterns of use of space over time associated with each pattern of work were identified. The results permitted a set of profiles of demand for environmental services to be developed, specific to each pattern of work in each type of building. Each pattern of work was identified as having typical ways of using space. Space layouts were built up from generic concepts for furniture and space use likely to support the different patterns of work.

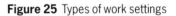

Den	Club
several simple settings	many rich complex settings
Hive	**Cell**
simple workstations	one rich complex setting

Figure 25 Types of work settings

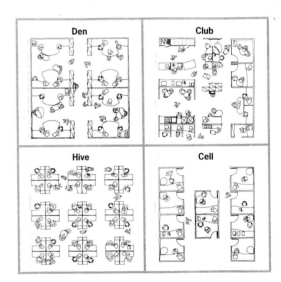

Figure 26 *Hive, cell, den,* and *club* space plans (source: DEGW)

Den	Club
• Group process work	• Varied work (individual and group)
• Low autonomy	• High autonomy
• High interaction	• High interaction
• PC, specialised equip	• Elaborate IT
• 9 to 5 hours, some variation	• Complex timetabling
Hive	**Cell**
• Individual process work	• Isolated work
• Low autonomy	• High autonomy
• Low interaction	• Low interaction
• Networked PC	• Laptop, networked PC
• 9 to 5 hours, shiftwork	• Individual timetabling

Figure 24 Work pattern characteristics

The characteristic settings to support the different patterns of work are also associated with expectations of the pattern of their use over time: the more interactive and more highly autonomous patterns of work are more likely to support the sharing of space over time (space use intensification) because the associated occupancy of space over time is likely to be intermittent or irregular. Higher levels of interaction and autonomy are also associated with the need for greater diversity of work settings. Moreover, such patterns of use are more likely to demand more elaborate environmental resources.

	Hive	Cell	Den	Club
Pattern of work	Work is broken down into the smallest components and carried out by staff who are given precise instructions and little discretion.	High level work carried out by talented independent individuals (isolated knowledge work).	Project or other group-work of a straightforward kind needing a changing balance of different, interdependent skills.	High level work carried out by talented independent individuals who need to work both collaboratively and individually: the work process is constantly being re-designed.
Occupancy of space over time, capacity for sharing space over time	Conventional 9 to 5, but tending towards shift work. The routine timetable, low interaction, and full time occupancy of space offer little scope for shared space use except through shift work.	Increasingly ragged and variable, more extended working days, depending on individual arrangements. If the occupancy of space is low then the opportunity exists for shared individual settings (whether enclosed or open).	Conventional 9 to 5, but becoming more varied by sub group activities. The opportunity for sharing space over time increases as interactive staff are more likely to be away from desks or out of the building.	Complex and dependent on what needs to be done and on individual arrangements, but expect high occupancy pattern of use over extended periods of time. Highly intermittent pattern of occupancy supports shared use of task settings.
Type of space layout	Open, ganged (4 or 6 pack), minimal partitions, maximal filing. Imposed simple space standards.	Highly cellular enclosed offices or highly individually used open workstations with high screening or partitions.	Group space or group rooms, medium filing. Complex and continuous spaces, incorporating meeting spaces and work spaces.	Diverse, complex and manipulable range of settings based on high variety of tasks. Space must be zoned for activities and planned to suit diverse use.
Use of IT	Simple dumb terminals or networked PCs.	Variety of individual PCs on networks and widespread use of laptops.	PCs and some shared specialised group equipment.	Variety of individual PCs on networks and widespread use of laptops. Range of tools for communication (video, audio).

Figure 27 Work pattern, space occupancy, layout and use of IT

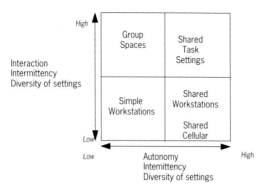

Figure 28 Patterns of space occupancy and the diversity of work settings

Examples of the assumptions used as part of the development of a series of databases on patterns of use are shown in the following tables. Several variations of the work patterns were tested to explore alternative scenarios involving different patterns of space layout and degrees of sharing of space over time.

For each scenario the following data were measured and compared:
- definition of size and types of space provided
- numbers of each type of setting provided across the typical floor;
- the sharing ratio of individual units of space (numbers of staff allocated to each space) if appropriate;
- the provision of IT equipment by type associated with particular work settings;
- the maximum number of people that the setting supports given the ratio of sharing;
- the % of gross floor area occupied by each type of work setting/activity;
- the hourly occupancy of each type of setting and associated pattern of use of IT at each setting across the 24 hour period;
- numbers of printers and other associated shared equipment such as copiers, coffee machines, mainframe computers, file servers, provided on the typical floor;
- the total space density and the total populations served by the typical floor.

The four examples shown in Figures 29–32 represent a cross-section of the variants examined, they are only one example of many possible solutions within each type of work pattern. The space densities are measured from the test layouts that were space planned onto the floors of the typical buildings. These densities therefore represent only one typical density as tested in the modelling exercise.

Note also that the term 'effective density' is used as a measure of density of occupancy to recognise where space use is shared over time. (For example, if two people share the same work setting, then the total effective density of the space occupancy is doubled). Densities were therefore calculated using the actual space layouts designed for the models, they distinguish between the space plan density (persons sqm/NIA*) and a total effective density which takes into account the degree of sharing of the space over time (persons sqm/NIA).

* net internal area

Hive

Organisational/ spatial type	Hive
Pattern of work	Routine repetitive consistent work undertaken by staff with little discretion or control over their work.
Typical organisations	Banking, information services, telesales, data processing.
Pattern of occupancy of space over time	Conventional working day, 9 to 5. But some tendency to shift work especially in intensive financial services and multinational organisations. Well established regular day time hours of occupancy and every staff member assumed to occupy a full-time workstation.
Typical scale	5-20 ✔ 20-100✔✔ 100-500 ✔✔✔ 500 + ✔✔✔ Large working groups 8-10-15; large total office populations.
Typical space use characteristics	High density 'six or eight packs' arranged in tight space planned framework. Highly standardised imposed layouts.

Typical floor
  Openness:
  Enclosure:
  Support space:
	
	80% (high)
	10% (low)
	10% (low)

Typical density
  Space plan:
  Total effective:
	
	10.5 sqm/person NIA
	10.5 sqm/person NIA (no shared space use assumed)

Potential for shared space use	Low, given expectation that everyone occupies their own space on a full time basis. (But some organisations will use shift working in which case the individual work space is used by two or three others over the day and the effective density is thereby greatly increased).
Use of IT	Maybe used extensively as in data entry and for routine information processing functions, likely to be terminals linked to mainframes, few laptops and PCs.
Implications for environmental servicing	In conventional *hive* offices expect highly serviced centrally controlled systems, single systems, integrated, with low levels of individual control.
Expectations for the future	Home working/tele-working may replace the *hive* office in some organisations. Some of this work may be exported to economies with low cost labour. Some may evolve towards *den* with higher interaction and a wider variety of work tasks. *Hive* may use more shift working.

Figure 29 Typical space use patterns for the *hive* work pattern (example from the research model).

Cell

Organisation/spatial type	Cell	

Pattern of work

Highly individual work performed at a high level by autonomous independent individuals. Characteristic work is isolated knowledge work without the requirement for high degrees of interaction. More likely to have a traditional status orientation, possibly with requirements for confidentiality and a stronger focus on quiet concentrated isolated work.

Typical organisations

Accountancy ('hotelling' offices), law, academia, research, software programming.

Pattern of occupancy of space over time

In the shared *cell* office, individuals occupy the office for irregular varied amounts of time, but may use the office for extended working days and well into the 24 hour period. The overall density of occupancy of the office will be high if sharing ratios are high.

Typical scale

5-20 ✔   20-100 ✔✔✔   100-500 ✔✔✔   500+ ✔✔✔

Large organisations will have the economies of scale suitable for managing and optimising a hotel-like service of space management.

Typical space use characteristics

Highly cellular enclosed office spaces in which the individual reserves space as in a hotel for a defined period of time. Personal files and accoutrements may be supplied to the room as required by the individual. Offices/workstations may be varied to suit whether the individual occupancy is for short or long duration (the touch down desk versus more long term use). Space sharing must be supported by extensive and well managed systems for storage (possibly mobile) and by clever phone routing (follow-me functions or cellular) as well as a sophisticated range of support spaces for meetings. Another option is to include highly screened workstations in an open plan layout.

Typical floor
  Openness: 0% (low)
  Enclosure: 70% (high)
  Support space: 30% (medium)

Typical density
  Space plan: 22.0 sqm/person NIA
  Total effective: 6.0 sqm/person NIA (assuming shared individual work settings in enclosed office space)

Shared space use

High

Use of IT

High levels of PCs and laptops networked to file servers. Localised specialised equipment available for complex IT work as required.

Implications for environmental servicing

The cellular space provides the maximum opportunity for high levels of individual control of the environment.

Expectations for the future

The growing needs for more interactive work may shift the *cell* towards the *club* type of environment; the full range of work and environmental problems cannot be solved in enclosed cells. The European Combi style offices anticipated these demands by providing smaller individual offices to achieve more shared resources.

Figure 30 Typical space use patterns for the *cell* work pattern (example from the research model)

Den		
	Organisation/spatial type	Den
	Pattern of work	Project or other kinds of group work of a straightforward kind requiring a mixture of different interdependent skills across a team or working group, mixture of interactive and individual work.
	Typical organisations	Advertising, architecture, design, media, engineering and others where project and team processes are significant.
	Pattern of occupancy of space over time	Conventional 9 to 5 but becoming varied by sub-group within the *den* office and by varied activities performed within the groups. The capacity for sharing space over time increases as the staff become more interactive or spend more time working outside the office.
	Typical scale	5-20 ✔ 20-100 ✔✔✔ 100-500 ✔✔✔ 500+ ✔✔✔
		Medium to large organisations in which group or team interaction is central to the work process.
	Typical space use characteristics	Group spaces, whether in group rooms or open-planned space, containing their own ancillary areas for meetings, interaction or shared equipment, usually continuous kinds of space.
	Typical floor *Openness:* *Enclosure:* *Support space:*	70% (high) 10% (low) 20% (medium)
	Typical density *Space plan:* *Total effective:*	14.7 sqm person/NIA 14.7 sqm person/NIA (It would also be possible to share *den* space under certain occupancy conditions)
	Potential for shared space use	Becoming higher as some groups spend more time working outside the office or at home and as the nature of their work becomes more interactive. Inter group, or cross team working may lead the *den* towards the *club* type of office.
	Use of IT	Variety of individual and group provision of IT, likely to include increasing provision of laptops and specialised equipment for shared use.
	Implications for environmental servicing	Simple or medium level provision of environmental services to serve a fairly regular pattern of daily use. Consensus required for group control.
	Expectations for the future	With more differentiation both within and between groups or teams, and as creative knowledge work increases in significance, the *den* may become a *club* type office.

Figure 31 Typical space use patterns for the *den* work pattern (example from the research model)

Club

Organisation/spatial type	Club: shared multi-activity settings.
Pattern of work	Transactional knowledge work. Highly interactive. Highly autonomous work in groups and teams, as well as concentrated individual work.
Typical organisations	Advertising, media, information technology, consultancy, and other high value adding sectors.
Pattern of occupancy of space over time	Extended working day and high density occupancy associated with shared use of space over time. Erratic and changeable occupancy pattern of individual and group settings within the office environment. Many staff spend much of their time out with clients and work at home part of the time.
Typical scale	5-20 ✔✔ 20-100 ✔✔✔ 100-500 ✔✔✔ 500+
Typical space use characteristics	Multi-activity settings have been used most often by smaller to medium sized organisations at any one site, probably due to the inherently complex space management required. Note that the floor area of the building can support a much higher number of staff in the organisation than the total number of work settings provided. This suggests that some smaller properties or lettings will become viable for larger organisational units that can work in this way.

High variety of types of task-based individual and group work settings. The settings are diverse, complex and manipulable. Traditional space standards (predicated on one person to a workstation) no longer apply. Space is planned and managed from an analysis of the work process and sharing ratios of people to settings. The traditional division between the workstation and ancillary and support space breaks down, support and ancillary spaces are dissolved within the general working area. Calculation of density has to be re-defined. Note that shared use of multi-activity settings still enables group space to be defined. |
Typical floor *Openness:* *Enclosure:* *Support space:*	40% (high) 20% (medium) 40% (high)
Typical density *Space plan:* *Total effective:*	17.0 sqm/person NIA 4.5 sqm/person NIA (assuming a high level of sharing of space).
Shared space use	High, and essential to make the system operable.
Use of IT	High levels of PCs and laptops networked to file servers. Localised specialised equipment available for complex IT work as required.
Implications for environmental servicing	Combination of highly serviced zones and other areas. High density occupancy characterised by extreme peaks and troughs in small zones. The control pattern should be simple and local to suit nomadic occupants who may not be familiar with the detailed layout and spaces of the building, but who will expect a high degree of temporary control over their changing work environment.
Expectations for the future	Increasingly used for core business and headquarters functions especially in expensive downtown locations. Elements may move to incorporate virtual offices via teleworking, telecommuting, video links.

Figure 32 Typical space use patterns for the *club* work pattern (example from the research model)

6.2 Modelling organisations into building types

The four buildings modelled in this way represented:
● an *atrium* building
● a *deep central core* building
● a *medium depth* building
● a *shallow depth* building

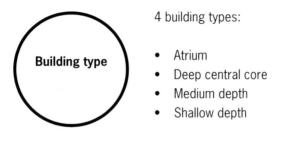

4 building types:

• Atrium
• Deep central core
• Medium depth
• Shallow depth

Figure 33 Four building types

The building types identified as being appropriate for the initial modelling exercise for the project have been chosen as types 1 - 4 defined in *ECON 19*, published by BRECSU (Building Research Energy Conservation Support Unit at BRE). They were described by BRECSU as:

Type 1   Naturally ventilated cellular (referred to here as *shallow depth*)
Type 2   Naturally ventilated open plan (referred to here as *medium depth*)
Type 3   Air conditioned standard (referred to here as: *deep central core*)
Type 4   Air conditioned prestige (referred to here as *atrium*).

These classifications arose from energy survey work carried out for the Energy Environment and Waste Office (now known as the Energy Directorate) in the 1980s. They are based upon an analysis of 400 office buildings (over 500 sqm) — with these four distinct types being identified as representative of the sample. Further survey work of 3000 buildings carried out by the Open University as part of the development of a UK non-domestic building stock model being undertaken by BRE and others on behalf of the DOE in the early 1990s confirmed that these four building types represented a good sample of the UK building stock.

It is important to emphasise that for the purposes of the NEW study the conventional associations between the base building shell type, the types of environmental servicing, and the assumed levels of specification are separated. The building types are considered purely as building shell types so that issues of appropriate environmental services and degree of appropriateness of the building type to the spatial demands of the organisation can be independently and separately evaluated. This is significant because the conventional understanding of the building type typically merges together issues of specification level, servicing type, and organisational demand into a hybrid description. For example, the *atrium* building is conventionally assumed to have a 'prestige' level of specification appropriate for certain kinds of users and to be serviced by full air conditioning. It is precisely such associations and assumptions that this study insists should be re-considered.

The profiles of the space and time use of each type of organisation (work pattern) in the four building types enabled the study to evaluate the potential of each building type to respond to the demands of the organisation. The modelling of each of the organisations involved the development of hypothetical space plans over a typical floor of each of the four building types. The results of the analysis are provided in Chapter 9.

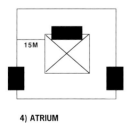

4) ATRIUM

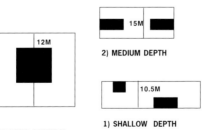

3) DEEP CENTRAL CORE

2) MEDIUM DEPTH

1) SHALLOW DEPTH

Figure 34 Four building types (diagrams)

7 The environmental system model

7.1 Evaluating environmental systems

From the generic description derived for each of the work patterns it is possible to consider how these might impact upon the specification of environmental systems. As previously explained, within this context we have taken the environmental systems to include HVAC (heating, ventilation, and air conditioning) systems and lighting systems.

Figure 35 summarises the requirements for HVAC systems; lighting is dealt with later in this chapter. As these requirements are based on generic work pattern descriptions they may at times appear simplified. Inevitably there will be exceptions to the system associations outlined here. However the derivation of the work pattern requirements for a specific building is an important step in the design process, and it is intended that the analysis described in this chapter will be adapted to suit individual circumstances. A more detailed consideration of affinities between HVAC system families (which are derived later in this chapter) and the four working patterns is provided in Chapter 10.

Den	Club
occasionally irregular day	irregular day
consistent	diverse spaces
team based control	enclosed / open mixture
consensus	varied demands
central / group systems	no ownership
	group / individual control
	high / low utilisation
Hive	**Cell**
regular day	irregular day
functional	individualistic spaces
predictable	unstable
consistent	highly services
low user control	responsive
central systems	individual control

Figure 35 Summary of environmental servicing demands associated with work patterns

HVAC servicing expectations

Hive

The *hive* is described as a mechanistic individual based workplace which will often consist of general functional workstations. The servicing system is not likely to be called upon to be highly responsive or flexible as *hive* tasks would be associated with a predictable stable environment. Given the relatively fixed day, uniformity of activity, and lack of intermittent occupation, a complex control strategy is unnecessary.

There would also be little (if any) expectation of individual control as a *hive* environment is associated with lack of autonomy, hence the use of central systems. This is not meant to imply that individual *hive* workers do not merit user control, it is simply stating that they are less likely to require it, or be given it, than their *cell, den,* or *club* counterparts. Reliance on natural ventilation alone may be insufficient to achieve the 'equality' of conditions and access to control required across the space.

Most *hive* work patterns would be expected to use an open planned space layout. Desk sharing is only likely if a pattern of shift working has been introduced. This would then extend the timetable of the building use. Over the standard day the occupancy density is likely to be greater than for the other working patterns unless the latter have initiated hot desking regimes to increase their effective density.

Cell

The *cell* is again described as an individualistic workplace, but with a much greater degree of autonomy and creativity involved. *Cell* workers are likely to have a more function dedicated workstation. They require a working environment which offers a greater opportunity for concentration, and possibly have a requirement for quiet spaces.

The *cell* worker will have greater expectations of a more highly serviced, high 'quality' environment (involving natural ventilation where possible) over which s/he is able to exercise a higher level of control than his or her *hive* counterparts. The preferred system must therefore be responsive, and have user-friendly local interfaces. The occupancy patterns will be more intermittent and variable than the *hive* as workers choose their own hours or work at weekends to suit the needs of the job.

The potential for space sharing is in theory high, but this will depend upon the degree of space personalisation required, and the specific patterns of use and occupancy. If it is introduced then space use intensification could lead to lower levels of diversity in space use occupancy as the number of free spaces would have been minimised.

Den

The *den* is an interactive team based workplace and is likely to have a variety of multi-function workstations. The working day may occasionally be extended to suit the needs of a particular project or team activity. As with the *cell*, a stimulating but focusing environment is required. A team may also require acoustic and visual privacy. There is the expectation of a highly serviced team space, with plant and control localised sufficiently to permit the initial selection and achievement of a team acceptable environment. It is anticipated that minimal interaction with the control would subsequently be required during occupancy. The suitability of natural ventilation may be affected by the variability of occupancy and occupation time between and within teams.

There is likely to be minimal personalisation but there could be a desire to register (temporary) team ownership of the space. Space use intensification is unlikely unless interaction or other activities increase outside the team area.

Club

The *club* is the most challenging of the four work patterns to service. It can potentially have any combination of the *cell*, *den* and *hive* features in its layout. Hence there will be an automatic inheritance of the expectations associated with the other constituent work patterns. Each of these will require the appropriate quality of environment, and possibly one which will allow the different work areas to be demarcated.

The *club* offers a high likelihood of shared space use and is also likely to be characterised by a high degree of churn. This dynamic pattern of use and lack of space ownership requires a 'universal' approach to the interfaces between the user and the environmental services to allow ease of use and instant familiarity. The space could have a mixture of high density areas and some with highly intermittent use such as specialised conference rooms.

7.2 Survey of industry opinion on HVAC system performance

Before continuing with the detailed evaluation of the various defined HVAC system families against work pattern requirements, a survey of wider industry perception of individual HVAC systems' performance strengths and weaknesses was undertaken. This was achieved through questioning representatives of five leading consulting engineers on their ratings of 18 different HVAC systems under 48 separate evaluation criteria.

The consultancies chosen are responsible for a major share of industry activity in the UK, and are reputed to represent diverse attitudes towards the use of passive and active building services systems. This evaluation took place without the consultants approached being aware of the work pattern definitions.

The 18 individual HVAC systems are described in Appendix A. Although this list is by no means comprehensive, the chosen systems demonstrate the available range of HVAC servicing options. Their subsequent grouping on completion of the survey into four HVAC system families is shown below.

The four families of HVAC systems

1 Distributed
- Four-pipe fan coil system with a central air handling unit
- Terminal heat pumps with a central air handling unit
- Induction units
- VRF cooling system
- ATM zonal

2 All air
- Variable air volume (VAV) with perimeter heating
- VAV with terminal re-heat
- Fan assisted VAV
- Dual duct air conditioning (constant volume – CV)
- Low temperature fan assisted VAV

3 Radiative air
- Mechanical displacement ventilation with static heating and cooling
- Ventilating chill/heat beam
- Mechanical displacement ventilation with perimeter heating
- Hollow core ventilation system

4 Tempered air
- Natural ventilation with perimeter heating
- Facade ventilation with perimeter heating
- Mechanical extract ventilation with window supply and perimeter heating
- Mechanical supply and extract with perimeter heating

The last category of *tempered air* was used within the confines of the industry survey but was then broadened to cover *mixed mode* systems as part of the wider analysis of affinities between HVAC systems, work patterns, and building types. The definitions and significance of *mixed mode* systems are explained in more detail in Chapter 10.

No grouping of HVAC systems can ever be perfect. It is recognised that within each family there will be systems which have unique qualities, or systems which are more advanced in certain areas than others. Examples of this are the ATM zonal system which allows maintenance outside of the occupied space, or the difference in performance at low duties between fan and non-fan assisted VAV systems. However within the context of this study definitions of families of systems greatly facilitated the analysis of the types of affinities discussed within the NEW study.

Each criterion could be scored on a basis of 0-100. Despite the range of organisational attitudes inherent within the survey responses, there was a high level of agreement between the markings given. To aid with the interpretation of trends from this mass of data, and so ease understanding of the systems' perceived performances, the 48 criteria were summarised into eight sets of issues. These are orientated around those features considered important within new working environments.

Ability of systems to provide specified environmental criteria

1 User
Summarises issues associated with user controllability, acceptance and the systems' ability to provide an environment perceived as comfortable.

2 Capacity
Concerns issues associated with the systems' ability to meet variations in heating and cooling demands, together with consideration of the precision with which these demands can be met.

3 Designability
Includes considerations associated with the robustness of the design in response to variations in the design conditions, ease of commissioning and the availability of design guidance.

Practical ease with which environmental criteria can be achieved

4 Integration
Represents the ease with which the system can be integrated into various space and building types, together with a consideration of the way in which the HVAC system impinges upon the selection and provision of other services.

5 Maintenance
Concerns issues associated with health and safety, down-time and ease of replacement or refurbishment of systems and their components.

6 Environmental
Looks at energy use and associated environmental impacts due to system selection and installation.

7 Life cycle costs
Costs associated with the selection, installation and operation of the particular HVAC system.

8 Innovation
Summarises the originality or leading edge nature of the system (as considered by experts within the field).

Upon creating these groups it became clear that seven of the eight sets of issues could be further grouped into two clusters. In essence, systems tended to be marked consistently in groups 1-3 and groups 4-7. Markings in the Innovation group 8 (not surprisingly) did not trend with either of the two clusters.

The emergence of this division of groups enabled the results of the survey to be succinctly summarised in the following system map, Figure 36. This is shown with the 'Y' axis representing the markings for groups 1-3 (indicating the potential ability of a system to provide the specified environmental criteria, eg technical performance issues) and the 'X' axis representing markings for groups 4-7 (indicating the ease with which this can be achieved eg cost and practicality).

The system map illustrates the industry's relative perceptions of the surveyed systems. The innovative labelling given to systems such as *displacement ventilation* is a reflection of the relative newness of such systems. There is the possibility that the industry's perceptions of their qualities may have been affected by a significant lack of first hand experience of their design and operation, thereby creating a tendency for cautious ranking of their attributes.

Ideal systems, that is those which permit maximum functionality in the most cost effective manner (as may be required by the *club* type environment), would tend towards the top right hand corner of the system map. None of the existing system families have been rated as offering this optimal solution. The arrows on the system map indicate the directions for improvement of each system family to meet the *club* requirements. However positioning on the map is not otherwise directly related to matching the requirements of other work patterns.

Based upon the survey findings and the project team's interpretation of the work pattern requirements for HVAC servicing, it is possible to identify 'failings' within each system family that would need to be rectified in order to meet these work pattern servicing demands. It is then also possible to identify directions for new products. This is discussed further in Chapters 18 and 19 where identified product developments are focused in several key areas, for example:

● *Controls*
The ability to respond to changing patterns of occupancy, increased levels of local control, and intelligent controls to minimise energy use.

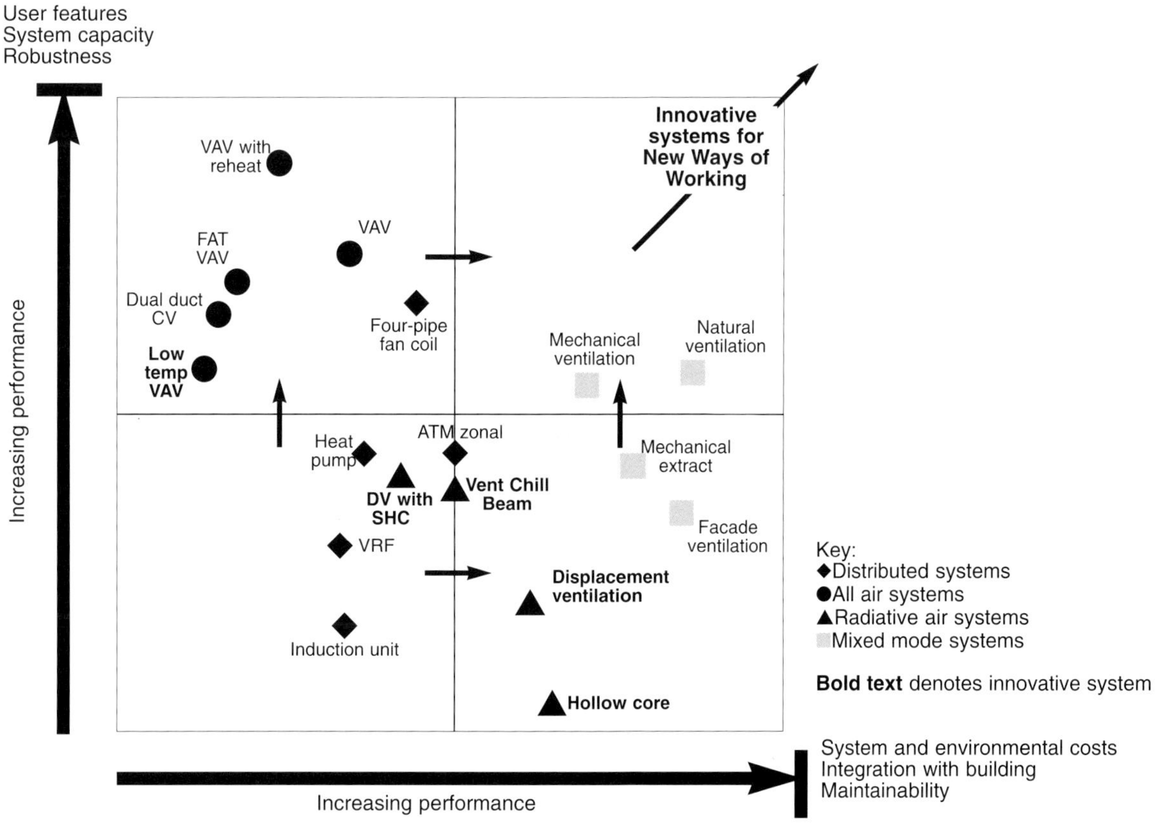

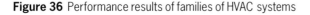

Figure 36 Performance results of families of HVAC systems

● *Maintenance*
Increased ease of maintenance, increased opportunity for maintenance outside of the occupied space, conditioned based maintenance, and automated fault detection.

● *Commissioning*
Self balancing systems, improved grille and diffuser design.

● *Modularity and flexibility*
Ease of upgrading and ease of re-design of HVAC systems.

7.3 Work pattern demands for lighting

Hive

The *hive* implies a sedentary and regular day although there could be expectations of shift work leading to either extended hours or 24-hour working. Tasks are workstation based and a high level of IT equipment could cause problems with glare and reflections. If offices are to make reduced use of paper, task lighting may become less necessary. The future implications of video work and emerging screen technologies needs to be kept in mind. Central shared support areas with highly focused special lighting will contrast with the workstation lighting set-up.

With the move to longer hours of occupation and night working there is the need to create variability and stimulation through the use of such techniques as sparkle and spot lighting in key areas, or changing light levels. To allow light to be reflected back into the space at night without cutting the occupant off from the outside world it may be necessary to develop blind systems or other window/lighting devices. Staff should, if possible, have access to daylight, or at least be able to have a sense of changing time or weather.

Cell

The *cell* requires an individual pattern of lighting with high levels of discretion and controllability to allow for highly varied and irregular use, although this will be difficult to address in situations where space sharing has been introduced, or when a *cell* is operating in an open plan space. The trend will be to allow an individual to set up the lighting system for the task which they are doing, and in their preferred manner. This requires a base level system of lighting to which equipment can be added.

Den

The *den* will consist of individuals who work based within a group of workstations supplemented by ancillary group/team/project facilities. All areas are likely to make use of IT equipment as well as paper. The space group ancillary areas may allow for the shared use of technologies such as video, projection, or special IT uses such as scanning which have particular lighting needs. Here the lighting can be used to emphasise and support changing activities. In the team ancillary areas task lighting may be appropriate.

Individual control of lighting can be provided by task lights within a team, with an associated level of ambient background lighting associated with the group. There may be problems with group consensus over the control of this background lighting.

Club

In the *club* the lighting is required to support individual and group activities with a varied occupancy pattern over time and shared ownership of settings. The need is for localisation and adaptability for changing tasks, preferences, and functions (both with and without VDUs) in the same space over time.

Users may not be familiar with the space or its control systems hence the latter must be intuitive and adaptable to their needs. Lighting should be used to differentiate between open interactive spaces and private enclosed individual areas. In the future individuals may carry with them their lighting preferences and programme the space to suit their needs. The building may provide standardised tools to access lighting (and other systems) which become familiar to everyone wherever they choose to work.

8　The cost model

8.1　Introduction

The development of a prototype life cycle costing model by Johnson Controls allowed us to determine the cost implications of a variety of fit-out elements within seven combinations of work patterns and building types. This chapter describes the derivation of the model, the assumptions made, and gives a discussion of the conclusions which the model was able to provide.

8.2　Cost study approach

The model was derived from the work pattern definitions used in Chapter 5. Typical costs were produced for a selection of building type / work pattern combinations as indicated in Figure 37. These combinations were chosen to cover the majority of the most well matched building type/working pattern affinities, ie those which were given the highest affinity rating as described in Chapter 9.

Building type	Hive	Cell	Den	Club
Atrium	•••	••	•••	•••
Deep plan	••	•	••	•••
Medium	•••	•••	•••	•••
Narrow plan	•	••	•	•••

Figure 37 Selected building type and work pattern combinations modelled in the cost study

8.3 Objectives of the cost study

The cost study objectives were to develop a conceptual generic model able to provide meaningful profiles of the economic relationships, on a life cycle basis, between work pattern and:
● building shell type
● installed HVAC family and category of lighting system
● type and quality of scenery and settings.
The cost model could only be developed at a basic illustrative level within this study. However it could ultimately be refined and extended to provide clients with a sophisticated decision making tool that could be tailored to their specific needs.

8.4 The model structure

The model has been developed in a matrix format using a standard spreadsheet calculation package. It examines the life cycle cost impact of various pairings of the seven building type and work pattern combinations previously referred to with an item drawn from one of the following five component classes:
● **Shell** type differentiating between the four building plan depths
● **HVAC** system type differentiating between the four system families (*all air, radiative air, distributed, mixed mode*)
● **Lighting** system type based on a selection from four options (passive/fixed grid, passive/variable grid, active/fixed grid, active/variable grid)
● One of three qualities of **scenery** (high, medium, low)
● One of three qualities of **settings** (high, medium, low) of furniture styles.

The results of the cost evaluations have been generated on a cost per head and cost per sqm basis, using *net present value* calculations based on a 10-year cycle with a discount rate of 9% (although the model includes the flexibility to change this). As is common convention the capital installation costs are represented in year 0, whereas annual and periodic maintenance costs commence in year 1. Costs presented in this study assume that reconfiguration of the HVAC systems, lighting, scenery and settings occurs every 10 years. This rate can be varied within the model.

Reconfiguration costs have been annualised for the HVAC and lighting systems. Exemplary cost data has been input from Johnson Controls' records database of their managed properties (*International Performance Management Database*, Johnson Controls) and other published sources which are listed in the References. Other key assumptions within the study have been listed within Appendix C of this book. It is recommended that they are referred to in order to fully understand the basis of the following results - in particular the assumptions made about the *mixed mode* systems.

8.5 Analysis of results and conclusions

As much of the data within the model comes from published sources or accepted norms, where any inaccuracies exist these are likely to be consistent across the work patterns, system types, building types, etc. Therefore, although the accuracy of the numbers cannot be assured, any patterns arising from the analysis can be assumed to indicate the generic concepts of the relative costs.

However, the case studies verify that in practice the costs of a single type of building housing a single type of work pattern can vary significantly depending upon the level of specification of the various components. In such cases the relative cost order could change significantly if comparisons of very low specification and very high specification buildings are made. These caveats notwithstanding the following discussion and analysis of the model results presents an interesting aspect of the impact of new ways of working.

There are some general points to note:
● The combined capital and installation costs are the dominant factors in all the life cycle calculations, contributing as much as 96% in the case of some building components.
● For all building types the combined costs of the scenery and settings significantly outweigh the costs of the building services or building structure.

A further dominant factor in the cost per head calculations is the effective density of the work pattern (*cell* 22.2 sqm/person, *den* 14.7 sqm/person, *hive* 10.4 sqm/person, *club* 7.6 sqm/person). The high effective density of the *club* derives from the assumed space sharing. Therefore overall life cycle costs per head rise with the work patterns from *club*, to *hive*, to *den* to *cell*. The one exception to this trend occurs in the comparison of high quality furniture where the pattern becomes *hive*, to *club*, to *den* to *cell*. This is due to the considerably higher cost of the high quality *club* furniture. It is however possible for other work patterns to involve a certain amount of space sharing resulting in a cost advantage.

Shell costs
The overall cost of the shell appears, from the limited data of this model, to increase in relation to the building type from *medium depth*, to *deep central core*, to *atrium* because of the increasingly complex structural requirements of the buildings.

The increased intensity of use of some of the work patterns causes very minor variations in the costs of fabric maintenance. A greater effect is noticeable for variations in the building types but even these are not significant.

HVAC systems
The *mixed mode* system offers the lowest life cycle cost solution in all the work pattern/building type combinations due to the high level of passive heating and cooling built into the system design and resultant reduction in plant costs from the assumption that a zoned *mixed mode* system is in place.

Of the building type/work pattern/HVAC system combinations costed, the lowest life cycle cost solution was a *mixed mode* system serving a *hive* environment in a *deep central core* building. The predominantly passive nature of

Figure 38 Shell costs per sqm

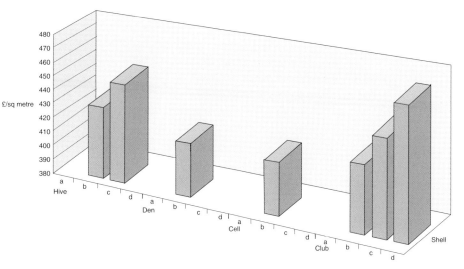

Shell - Cost per square metre

Figure 39 Shell costs per head

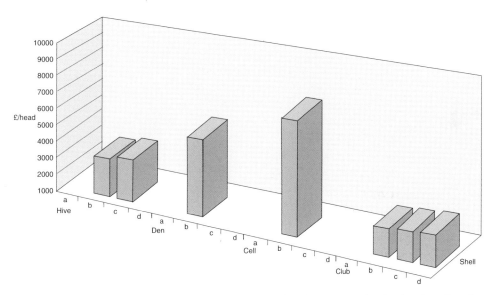

Shell - Cost per head

the *mixed mode* design in conjunction with the low level of user control required for a *hive* environment contribute to low costs in many areas of the model. However, other factors such as the ease with which a large volume space with a constant load can be controlled also has an effect on these low life cycle costs.

The *radiative air* and *mixed mode* systems show lower utilities costs than those of the *distributed* systems and *all air* systems. With the *mixed mode* systems this is due to the increased dependence upon natural ventilation. In the case of the *radiative air* systems this is partly explained by certain members of this family treating (ie cooling, or humidifying) only sufficient fresh air to meet the needs of the occupants, with the remainder of the cooling load being met more efficiently by a water

based distribution method. The *distributed* system has particularly high utilities costs due to the assumed reduced efficiency achievable with small HVAC components.

The *mixed mode* systems show lower maintenance costs than the *distributed*, *all air* and *radiative air* systems. These can be attributed to the lower levels of mechanical components within these systems and reduced wear and tear. The *distributed* systems have the highest maintenance costs because of the higher number of units containing maintainable items.

There appears to be a general trend across the majority of the HVAC system cost components increasing from *hive*, to *club*, to *den*, to *cell*. The only cost component which does not follow

Figure 40
HVAC - Cost per sqm

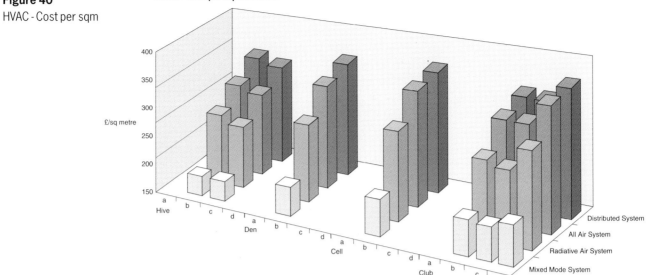

HVAC - Cost per square metre

Figure 41
HVAC - cost per head

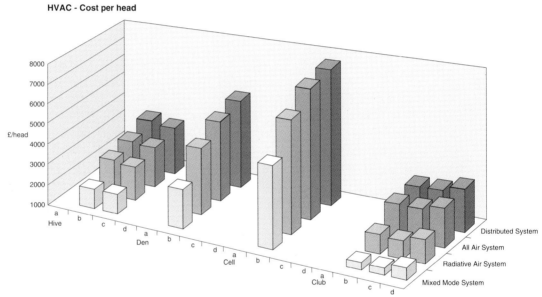

HVAC - Cost per head

this pattern is the utilities costs. However, the utilities costs are a significant enough component to ensure that the general trend in the capital and installation, maintenance and reconfiguration costs is not replicated in the total HVAC costs. Instead, the *radiative air* and *all air* systems have increasing overall life cycle costs from the *hive*, to *club*, to *den* to *cell*; whilst the *distributed* systems increase from *club*, to *hive*, to *den* to *cell*; and the *mixed mode* systems increase from *hive*, to *den* to *club* to *cell*.

The *cell* environment is comparatively expensive due to higher capital, installation and maintenance costs resulting partly from the higher densities of air treatment units or supply and extract ducting. However, the high quality environment and the high level of user control expected within this environment will also be a contributing factor.

Lighting
The variable grid lighting systems have significantly greater capital and installation costs than the fixed grid systems. Whilst the cost of reconfiguring a variable grid system is only 10% of that of a fixed grid system, with a reconfiguration rate of 3 times in 10 years these savings do not offset the additional capital and installation costs. Taking the *medium depth* building as an example, savings from the variable grid system do not accrue until the reconfiguration rate reaches 8 times in 10 years for an active system in a *cell*, 9 times in 10 years for a passive system in a *cell*, and 10 times in 10 years for a passive system in a *hive*. The *club* and *den* work patterns do not achieve any savings during the 10 year life cycle in this building type.

The *deep central core* building has a significantly greater overall life cycle cost across all four lighting system categories than the other building forms. This results from higher utilities and maintenance costs due to the permanent artificial lighting requirement towards the centre of the building during the occupancy period.

The *medium depth* building and the *atrium* building have very similar costs due to a similar lighting requirement. The light well effect of a central atrium enables daylight penetration from the atrium as well as the exterior facade, resulting in a similar daylight: artificial lighting ratio as that of the *medium depth* building.

The *cell* work pattern has lower utilities costs than the other working patterns as occupants in a non-shared *cell* are more likely to turn off the lights when they are not needed. However, the additional wiring and switching required to provide occupancy control of the cellular areas causes the capital, installation and maintenance costs to be higher for the *cell* work pattern than for other work patterns.

The *deep central core* building with a variable active grid lighting system and housing a *hive* environment offers the highest overall life cycle cost solution. The scope for absence detection control within a *hive* environment is minimal whilst any daylight control around the

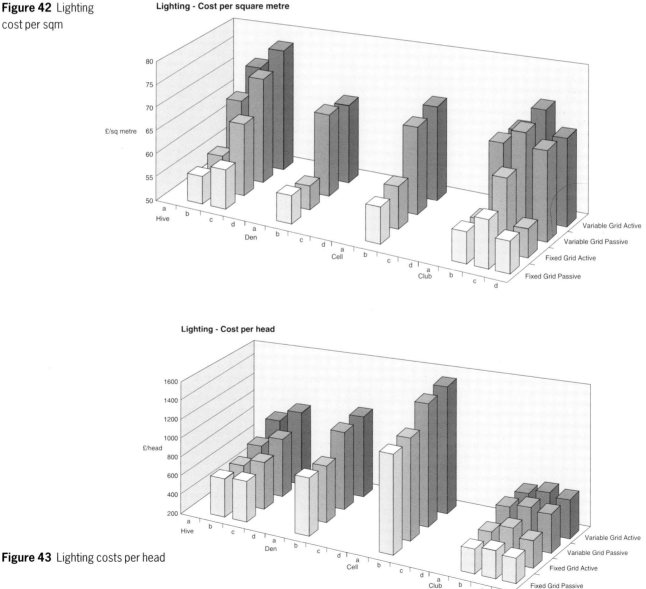

Figure 42 Lighting cost per sqm

Figure 43 Lighting costs per head

perimeter of a *deep central core* building is only going to contribute very small savings when averaged across the whole building area. Therefore the potential benefits of an active lighting system are not realised within this work pattern/building type combination.

Scenery

There appears to be a trend of overall life cycle costs increasing from *medium depth* building, to *deep central core* building, to *atrium* building. The additional structural requirements of the *deep* or *atrium* buildings increases the likelihood of having to fit scenery components around columns, etc. This causes an increase in the capital and installation costs. Higher capital and installation costs contribute to a high

overall life cycle cost for the *cell* work pattern. These result from increased partitioning in the *cell* environment. The opposite effect is found with the *hive* environment where minimal partitioning leads to lower capital and installation costs and hence lower overall life cycle costs.

Settings

Furniture costs are dependent on work pattern and furniture quality but not on building type.

Costs increase from *hive* to *den* to *cell* to *club* as the specification of a typical workstation increases (eg from a bench, to an L-shape, to system furniture, to system furniture with additional social support furniture).

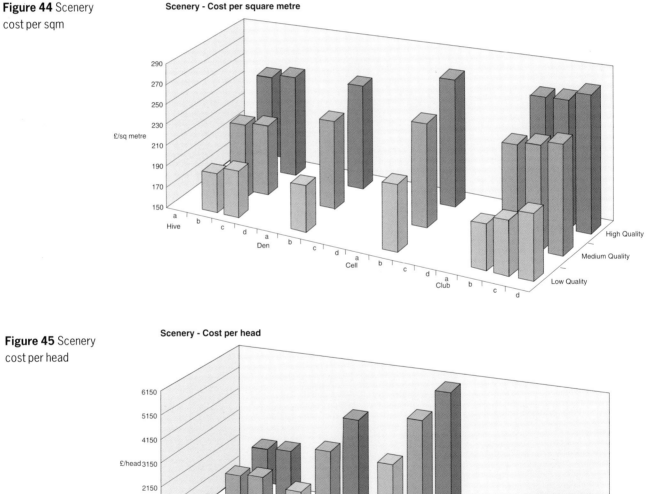

Figure 44 Scenery cost per sqm

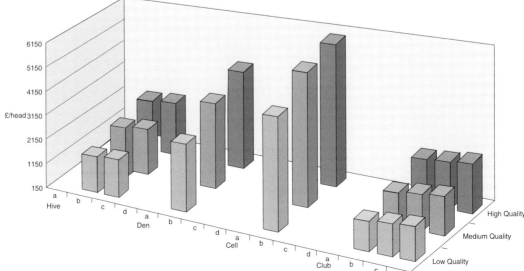

Figure 45 Scenery cost per head

Figure 46 Setting - cost per sqm

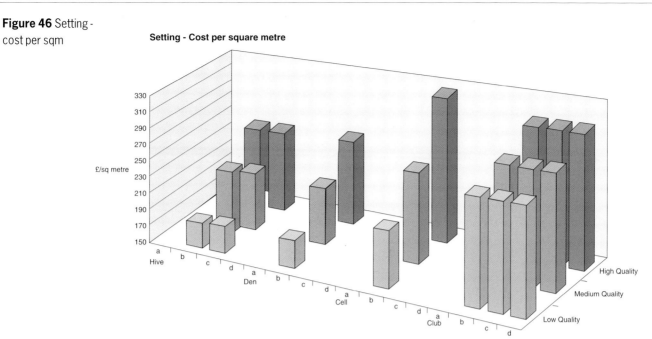

Figure 47 Setting - cost per head

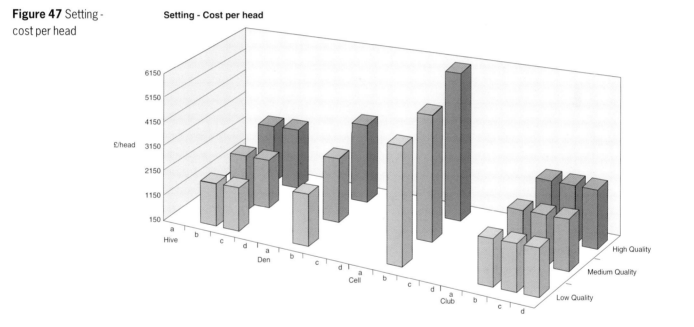

Part 3: Affinities between work patterns, building types and environmental systems

Part 1

Part 2

Part 3

Part 4

Part 5

Bibliography and appendices

The idea of 'affinity' has been developed to first describe, and then evaluate, how well the demands of work patterns are met by different HVAC systems and building types. The strengths and weaknesses of the HVAC systems and building types are highlighted in a simple way. The definition of sets of affinities between work patterns, building types, and HVAC systems is also used to indicate where opportunities exist for developers, designers, suppliers and manufacturers to improve their products to better match varied and emerging user needs. These affinities are explored in sequence:

- work patterns: building types
- work patterns: HVAC systems
- HVAC systems: building types.

Finally, a review of the dynamics of change implicit in the model of work patterns and organisations is used to identify which HVAC systems, in which kinds of buildings, are most likely to match users' needs.

9 Affinities between the work patterns: building types

Introduction: the idea of affinities

The term 'affinity' is used in the study to describe and evaluate the significant differences of how well the work pattern demands are met by both building types and environmental services. The measure of affinity in this sense is the degree to which the complex demands of the work patterns (*hive, cell, den* and *club*) are achieved (or not), how far they are resolved, and how satisfactorily they can be accommodated in different building types (*atrium, deep central core, medium depth, shallow depth*); as well as differences between how well different families of environmental systems can support these demands (*distributed, all air, radiative air*, and *mixed mode*) in those different building types.

In this sense 'affinities' describe the inherent quality and appropriateness of the relationships between the types of patterns of work, the building types and the families of environmental systems. A good affinity (or set of affinities) suggests a greater likelihood that needs will be satisfied between the work pattern, the building, and the HVAC system in question.

The examination of these affinities is thereby a means of defining the inherent match or fit between user characteristics, HVAC system attributes, and simple building type characteristics, in order to optimise solutions. The idea of affinity is defined by the current status of knowledge of user requirements and of the technical and spatial features of buildings and HVAC systems. The notion of affinities is therefore by its nature a broad brush evaluation and one that will inevitably change with time.

Thus, there will be affinities between the organisational types and the building types. Furthermore there are expected affinities between the building types and the types of HVAC servicing systems which are likely to be most appropriate. The evaluation and definition of these sets of affinities is a central purpose and basis of the research. The key findings are explored in the following sections.

The point here is not to use either the models of organisations or the building types in a deterministic way, but as a device for elucidating critical differences in the relationships between the organisation, its use of space and buildings over time, and its associated demands for HVAC services. The definition of these sets of affinities is also a means of alerting users, designers and manufacturers to the potentialities of systems, or buildings, to solve certain kinds of user demands. It also alerts the same people to the risks of supplying technologies and buildings that may fail. It thereby also provides us with a means of defining ways in which buildings and systems need to be improved and better provided to meet the needs of users.

The end result is an understanding of the strengths and weaknesses of the performance of the existing range of typical HVAC systems in responding to the demands of a range of types of organisations in various building types. Directions of change for the future are then identified as likely to improve the performance of these HVAC systems. These can be used both to highlight technical changes required in the servicing systems as well as to indicate the ways in which we see building shell design and specification evolving to support such changes in technology and organisational behaviour. The affinities also suggest ways in which the findings can be used by those with different interests, whether the developer, the user, the manufacturer or designer. The implications for these particular interest groups are highlighted in Chapters 17, 18, 19, 20.

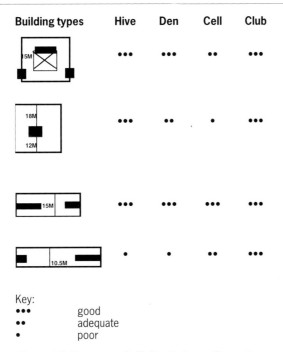

Key:
- ••• good
- •• adequate
- • poor

Figure 48 Summary of affinities between the work patterns: building types

The atrium building type

At 15m glass to glass, this building type works very well for all organisational types except for the *cell* work pattern in an enclosed space layout. In the conventional building types available in the UK it would normally be the case that the *atrium* building would be considered over-specified for use by *hive* types of organisation. For *den* organisations this building type is well suited in providing a combination of team and ancillary spaces across the floors with high levels of connectivity. For the *cell* organisation with high levels of enclosure the *atrium* building type may be overly deep if all offices are to have aspect, but works well if some interior space is used for ancillary and support functions; for an open planned *cell* layout (where workstations are highly screened for individual concentrated work) the depth is not so much of a problem. For the *club* organisation, the variety of shared group and individual spaces can be very well accommodated, deeper spaces are well suited for occasional use by individuals or groups for equipment and support spaces.

The deep central core building type

The uniform open space with greater depth is well suited to the *hive* organisation. For the *den*, the deep internal space of the building type may be difficult to use for working groups.

For the *cell* organisation the depth of space is too deep for most enclosed offices to have aspect; it is likely to be overly deep even for an open planned *cell* organisation. For the *club* organisation the variety of shared group and individual spaces can be very well accommodated, the deeper spaces are well suited for occasional use by individuals or groups, or for equipment and support spaces.

The medium depth building type

As with the *atrium* building type above this will work well for all organisational types except that the core locations make this building shape easier to use for enclosed *cell* organisations.

The shallow depth building type

The *shallow depth* building type does not work well for the *hive* organisation or *den* given the size of working groups and degrees of interaction likely to be required. For *cell* and smaller *club* organisations the space provides high levels of aspect, but the range of settings required in both the larger *club* and *cell* organisations for support and ancillary functions make this plan less effective overall than the *medium depth* space.

10 Affinities between the work patterns: environmental systems

10.1 Summary of major affinities between the work patterns and the environmental systems

This chapter looks at the affinities between the work patterns and both HVAC and lighting systems. Figure 49 provides a simple and effective way of understanding the most natural affinities between the work pattern, the HVAC systems, and different types of space layout (an open plan versus a cellular space layout is indicated where relevant for each work pattern). This reference to cellular is not to be confused with the *cell* work pattern. In this context it means an environment which is either divided by full height or very high partitions. The explanations for these affinities are given in the next few pages.

There are several reasons why the lines drawn in Figure 49 are fuzzy rather than absolute. Firstly, as previously stated these are affinities and are therefore only indicators of the level of appropriateness of the system for the work pattern. The affinity ratings are intended to provide a reasonable match between what is necessary to operate effectively, what can practically be provided, and what is likely to be expected. The work pattern expectations discussed in this chapter are not intended to indicate that a member of staff operating in one working pattern is entitled to a better quality of environment than another. It should also be re-iterated here that many buildings will be operating well with a servicing system shown here as having a poor affinity, and vice versa. Affinities are given here as a starting point for debate between the client and design team.

Secondly HVAC systems are constantly under development; for example if an *all air* system could be designed to have the same general capabilities as a *distributed* system, ie enhanced user control, then its position within the diagram would change.

Thirdly, individual systems within each family will have unique or enhanced features, eg fan assisted terminal reheat VAV versus the standard VAV system. However Figure 49 is seen as a useful way of depicting the current major affinities between the expectations of work patterns and the ability of HVAC systems to deliver suitable environments for them. Note that the *tempered air* system family is now referred to as *mixed mode*. *Mixed mode* systems are explained in more detail later in this chapter. Basically they consist of an HVAC system which combines natural and mechanical ventilation solutions (*tempered air*), possibly with some cooling or air conditioning, in the most beneficial way. As a result any member of the other system families could, in theory, appear as part of a *mixed mode* solution. As the variety of *mixed mode* solutions is infinite it was not possible to consider them as a separate category in the industry survey carried out to generate Figure 36 in Chapter 7. However it is possible to consider the general attributes of these systems in the context of developing affinities.

The following definitions have been developed as part of other research undertaken by BRE to illustrate the variety of *mixed mode* strategies used:

● Contingency systems
In its most common form it is a building designed to be naturally ventilated, but which also has a clear plan for adding mechanical ventilation and/or cooling at a later date. Buildings designed in this way are relatively few. Either space will be allowed for in the building into which active systems can be installed at a later date, or such systems will be disabled until required, eg if cooling loads increase due to additional occupancy or increased IT loads.

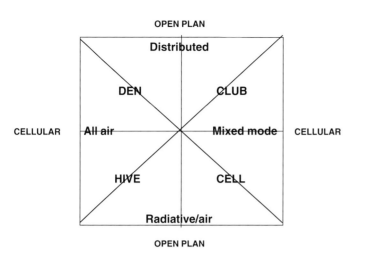

Figure 49 Affinities between the work patterns and environmental systems with different degrees of enclosure of space layout

● Concurrent systems
These are the most common form of hybrid system where the mechanical plant operates in conjunction with opening windows. Often systems are designed so that the mechanical systems are sufficient to provide good indoor air quality, remove heat and control draughts. The opening windows act as an optional extra for the benefit of the occupants.

● Changeover systems
Natural and mechanical systems are available and used as alternatives according to need, but not at the same time. An example of this might be seasonal changeover where, in the mild weather of spring and autumn, windows are opened. During the winter windows may be sealed and the building mechanically ventilated. During the summer comfort cooling may be provided, again with the windows sealed. Local changeover systems may incorporate window detectors to switch off nearby air conditioning or comfort cooling units when windows are opened.

● Zoned systems
Differing servicing methods are provided in different zones of the building. By this we do not include those special areas of the building where some form of mechanical assistance is generally required, eg toilets or meeting rooms.

The *mixed mode* strategy adopted will have an impact on the choice of suitable HVAC system. For example, systems which rely more on

radiative heat exchange are less affected by fluctuations in the air movement through open windows than systems based on convective heat transfer. Hence a Hollowcore system can be used in a concurrent mode of operation more easily than a VAV system. However, other members of the *radiative air* systems which incorporate a low air flow displacement ventilation element may find that this is more affected by opening windows. With a changeover system interaction with opening windows would not be an issue as the two would never operate in parallel.

Design guidance for *mixed mode* buildings is still developing and the reader is referred to the Bibliography for details of further reading.

Hive
The open planned *hive* has an affinity with the *radiative air* systems, given the limited need for localised control required to match the expectations of staff, and to avoid confrontation arising from the unequal provision of controls, eg people seated away from, as opposed to close to, windows. These systems are well suited to dealing with the consistent loads and limited diversity requirements of the *hive*. The radiative component is regarded as providing a high level of comfort, with displacement ventilation claimed to provide high air quality for lower air volumes. This potential energy saving is beneficial in the *hive* where there is limited opportunity to make savings through intermittent occupancy.

It is unlikely that the cellular *hive* arrangement will occur as most *hives* are in large open plan spaces. It is, however, possible that small *hive* areas could occur. *All air* systems would appear to offer sufficient control to cope with the minimal diversity expected from the *hive*, but with the potentially smaller zone sizes needed to match the degree of enclosure. Depending upon the number of people occupying each space, interaction problems may occur due to differing requirements for comfort. The development of some form of polling or averaging control via a PC interface could be of benefit to prevent confrontation over issues of control. This could either be used within a space or across a number of spaces depending upon the system zoning.

Cell

The open planned *cell* has an affinity to *radiative air* systems. Even though the cell worker would have an expectation of localised individual control whenever possible, this is not really viable with any of the four family systems within an open planned space. Even *distributed* systems can find it difficult to offer localised control (unless personal desk ventilators are proven to work) because of their zone size and system interaction problems.

Mixed mode may not be as effective in the open planned space because of preferential seating consequences and the impact of control decisions. High quality *radiative air* systems give a consistent environment and it may be possible in the future to provide radiative elements with some individual control (as in lighting). However, unless space sharing has been introduced *radiative air* systems may not be able to adapt as beneficially to the savings to be made from intermittent occupation as *distributed* systems. *Radiative air* systems do, however, avoid the need for complex controls which may be unfamiliar to those entering an unfamiliar space.

The enclosed variant of *cell* has an affinity with *mixed mode* systems. Within the UK, at least, surveys have indicated that people prefer natural ventilation whenever possible (ie suitable climate, location). Solutions to maximise the use of natural ventilation will be preferred by creative individuals in their own work spaces where the decision to open a window will have no impact on their colleagues.

Den

The open planned variant of the *den* work pattern has an affinity with *distributed* systems in that they offer the best option for satisfying the diverse demands of the teams and providing local controls. Systems can operate with a lower quality and a larger zone solution in the case of open planned *dens* than for open planned *clubs*. The preferred design of the system is dependent upon the degree of mobility of the team in the work space. The purpose of the systems is to support and reinforce the team or group identity yet also to maintain a consistent environment to minimise conflict within the team space.

The cellular variant of *den* (ie group offices for 6+ people) has an affinity with *all air* systems, as they are able to cope with the inherent diversity of such an arrangement which is not as great as for a cellular *club*. System control should be linked to levels of occupancy if there is likely to be significant variation within the team. For smaller offices, the *mixed mode* approach can work well providing there is no conflict over window opening.

Club

The more open planned variant of the *club* office has an affinity with *distributed* systems. These offer the best opportunity to satisfy diverse demands (both occupancy levels and erratic working hours) and offer localised control. Functional identity can be varied by offering contrasting servicing levels through both the HVAC system and the lighting.

The more cellular version of the *club* has an affinity with *mixed mode* systems. The logic is similar to that of the cellular *cell* environment but is even more appropriate because of the requirements for flexibility. The slower speed of response and lesser ability to cope with diverse high loads reduces the appropriateness of the *radiative air* systems for the *club* users.

In an ideal situation every individual would have total control over their environment from a HVAC and lighting perspective. This is however impractical for both economic and technical reasons. Indeed Figure 49 suggests that contrary to received wisdom, the most creative workplaces (*club*) have the highest affinity with the potentially lower cost HVAC systems (*mixed mode*). Whereas the simpler *hive* and *den* working styles, traditionally housed in naturally ventilated buildings, have the greatest affinity with the nominally more serviced and sophisticated *radiative air* system. This is a reversal of traditional thinking which would be to locate the *hive* work pattern in a cheaper, more simply serviced environment.

	All air	Radiative air	Distributed	Mixed mode
Hive (open)	••	•••	••	•
Hive (closed)	•••	••	••	••
Den (open)	••	• (+• if static dens)	•••	• (+• if high partitioning)
Den (closed)	•••	•	••	••
Cell (open)	••	•••	••	•
Cell (closed)	••	• (+• if improved local control and limited diversity)	••	•••
Club (open)	••	•	•••	•
Club (closed)	••	•	••	•••

Key:
••• good
•• adequate
• poor

Figure 50 Affinities between work patterns and HVAC systems

10.2 Other HVAC system affinities

This analysis of HVAC systems was taken further to derive the affinity ratings for the remaining work pattern and HVAC system combinations. Those combinations highlighted in Figure 49 as major affinities score three in Figure 50.

Note that it is possible within any one system family to have a high or low quality system in its own right. The reasoning behind the choices given here relates to the inherent quality of the system to meet certain demands, not to its installed quality, nor to the care with which it is operated.

All air systems offer a compromise solution across many of the work patterns in that they provide some degree of flexibility and can be zoned sufficiently small to suit most situations (open plan or cellular). They do not currently offer the same potential degree of user control as *distributed* systems making them slightly less suited to the *club* and *cell*.

Distributed systems by their nature are inherently flexible and able to be controlled to cope with diversity. Hence they score well in open plan *clubs* and *dens*. Unless personal desk ventilators (or similar) become more viable, *distributed* systems will not readily be zonable on an individual basis in an open plan space for a *cell* environment.

Radiative air systems are not as readily flexible as the previous systems and therefore score highest with the open *hive*. Their use with the

open *den* is dependent upon the static properties of the occupants of the *dens*. They may be more viable in the closed *cell* should user control be improved.

The success of *mixed mode* systems is dependent upon the degree of access to openable windows and the likelihood of conflict, hence the lower scores given for this system family in open plan environments. They score higher in the more dynamic *cell* and *club* environments as the preference for natural ventilation with high levels of user control can be accompanied by the flexibility of the installed mechanical systems which may be *distributed*, *all air* or *radiative air* depending upon the strategy used.

Lighting system affinities

The *hive*, *cell*, *den*, and *club* are associated not only with typical kinds of space layout but also with patterns of owned, shared, and temporarily occupied patterns of use. The models of the work patterns suggest the potential for the sharing of space over time across all of the four types but with some key differences. In the *hive* work pattern the sharing of space over time is typically associated with shift work (diachronic). In the *cell*, *den*, and *club* other simultaneous patterns of sharing or space use intensification are possible (synchronic).

BRE and William Bordass have explored some of the lighting design and control implications associated with differing patterns of space management. These have been placed into the context of the *hive*, *den*, *cell* and *club* model in Figure 51.

Space management	Work pattern	Space layout	Pattern of sharing
Owned	Cell	open plan or enclosed	NA
	Hive	open plan	NA
Temporarily owned	Hive	open plan	shift work
	Cell	open plan or enclosed	time share
	Den	open plan or group room	time share
	Club	open plan or enclosed	time share
Shared	Den	open plan or group room	shared space

Figure 51 Space management, work patterns, space layout and pattern of sharing

Space ownership	Characteristic	Examples	Typical issues and problems	Suitable approaches
Owned	Occupants regard the space as their own and want to make all the decisions about the status of their lights. A close relationship between user, space and control makes this possible.	Small offices for 1 and 2 persons.	Occupants need to switch both on and off, and greatly object to 'Big Brother' controls. Any automatic adjustments should be imperceptible to them.	Avoid automatic light switch-on. Light switches by the door can be used effectively. Consider absence-seeking and gradual dimming to avoid waste and annoyance. Always provide local override.
Shared	Occupants regard their space as their own, but cannot be in full control of environmental systems which have to suit others as well. Ideally there should be some local control, or failing that task lighting available on request.	Open-plan offices and group rooms.	Systems default to convenient but inefficient states, typically with all the lights on. The status then only changes if the situation becomes intolerable, or at the end of the day.	Separate control (and identification) of lighting for circulation, decoration and safety avoids the first arrival switching on everything. Ideally local switching and adjustment are available at individual workstations. A 'last out, lights out' facility could be used.
Temporarily owned	Occupants are usually present for a few hours at a time. They can be in individual or consensus control while they are there, but they may not be very familiar with the controls. Lights may left on when the rooms are vacated as nobody feels responsible.	Meeting rooms, quiet rooms, study carrels, laboratory writing-up areas, project areas.	Controls are not easy to find or understand. Presence detection is mis-used in meeting rooms by omitting local override for slide presentations, etc. Nuisance triggering of presence detectors can occur. Manual 'on' is often preferable.	Highly visible, intuitive local controls are needed in obvious places. Absence detection is desirable preferably with 'last out, lights out' facility at the exit. Teaching and presentation rooms may require dimming and control from the lectern.

Figure 52 Implications of space ownership and management for lighting (source: William Bordass)

11 Affinities between the HVAC systems and building types

11.1 Summary of affinities

A table of affinities was also derived (Figure 53) between HVAC systems and building forms independent of the work pattern. Of all the affinity tables this is, of necessity, the fuzziest in that circumstances can vary so much between buildings of a particular form. Also HVAC systems have deliberately been developed to suit a large number of building types, hence differences in suitability of systems are more difficult to define and cannot fail to be largely subjective. Again at this point we must stress the necessity of adapting this analysis method to particular situations. However, a brief explanation of how we derived this table may assist in this.

11.2 All air systems

All air systems are seen as being equally as well suited on average to *deep central core* and *atrium* buildings, but are not the first choice system in either the *medium depth* or *shallow plan* relative to the other system families.

11.3 Radiative air systems

It is less likely that air conditioning or comfort cooling would be required within a *shallow plan* building. One reason may be to achieve uniformity against consistent loads across the space, for which a *radiative air* solution may work. Within the *medium depth* building where mechanical servicing is likely to be more appropriate the affinity rating can be increased, similarly for the *deep central core* and *atrium* buildings.

11.4 Distributed systems

If a *shallow plan* building requires localised spot cooling this could be achieved most easily through the introduction of units from a member of the *distributed* family which could be located on the perimeter wall with a ready source of fresh air to each. The affinity rating increases in the *medium depth* building as above. However the *distributed* systems score slightly less in the *atrium* building than the other building types as they could not benefit from it as a source of fresh air.

11.5 Mixed mode systems

Mixed mode systems appear to score well for every building type. This is a reflection of their ability to meet a wide range of demands due to the variety of design and operation strategies which can be used, eg contingency, changeover, zoned as discussed in Chapter 10.

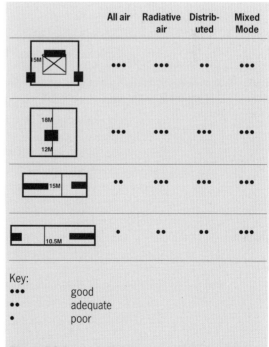

	All air	Radiative air	Distrib-uted	Mixed Mode
(15M)	•••	•••	••	•••
(18M / 12M)	•••	•••	•••	•••
(15M)	••	•••	•••	•••
(10.5M)	•	••	••	•••

Key:
•••   good
••   adequate
•   poor

Figure 53 Table of affinities between HVAC systems and building forms independent of the work pattern

12 Optimal overall affinities between the work patterns, the building types and the HVAC systems

12.1 Optimal affinities

Three critical relationships that determine the quality and performance of HVAC systems required by users have been examined:

- the work patterns: building types
- the work patterns: HVAC systems
- the HVAC systems: building types.

For each of these relationships, a series of tables has been prepared that highlight relative performance in a simple way. They are presented in the following pages. They provide a means of focusing on areas that require product development, as well as those that are already successful and do not require attention. They illustrate a range of possible actions that may be taken depending on the needs and interests of the reader. They indicate likely affinities between the three factors of work pattern, building type and HVAC system. They are not intended to be prescriptive as so many other factors will come into play in the case of any one individual building.

The developer or property holder

For example, a developer or a major property holder may be interested to consider the potential flexibility range of building types in their portfolio or which they may be intending to develop. The tables assist in highlighting which building types appear most appropriate to serve the needs of a range of organisational types and which HVAC systems appear most able to solve the needs of these organisational types within certain kinds of buildings.

For example, using the tables, we can see that a developer or property holder wishing to maximise the attractiveness of his building stock to the market will prefer to develop or hold the *medium depth* or *atrium* building types,

as these are most suitable for the widest range of organisational types investigated; *deep central core* and *shallow depth* buildings being less often suitable. Furthermore, given a stock of existing *medium depth* buildings, and assuming that the developer may wish to ensure that they are suitable for the burgeoning users in *den* and *club* type organisations, the families of HVAC systems which would be most suitable are: *distributed* and *mixed mode*.

The suppliers

For the supplier of environmental services systems, interiors, furniture and settings, the tables suggest how well different building types and system types will serve the needs of different kinds of users. They also indicate which are the key problem areas to be further investigated to understand where there are particular failures: should the product be re-thought, is it inappropriate for certain users or certain building types?

For example, the suppliers of *radiative air* systems may note that although their types of systems appear to well suit the *deep central core* building type, and work well for *hive* organisations; they do not work as well for other organisational types such as the *den*, this organisational type in turn is less well suited to the *deep central core* building type. Can these systems be re-designed to better suit other kinds of user demands and to better fit with other kinds of buildings?

The users

For the user, the tables enable selection of building types and HVAC servicing systems to be seen in the context of their own organisational characteristics: as a *den* or *club* organisation, which type of buildings and systems offer the least risk and the greatest capacity to achieve what is needed? Which buildings and systems should be avoided?

For example, an organisation that defines itself as predominantly *den,* but has the intention of moving towards innovative space sharing arrangements and more interactive knowledge work processes, will wish to select buildings and environmental systems that will support its transition towards the *club* type of office. The tables suggest they avoid: *deep central core* buildings (as a *den*) and that as a future *club* they may want to select building types such as *atrium* or *medium depth* which would suit the *mixed mode* or *distributed* families of HVAC systems in the longer term. Chapter 13 further outlines what may be some optimum shifts between HVAC system types to suit changing organisational demands of this kind.

The tables also enabled the project team to focus their attention on some wider implications:
- the implications for the design of the base building and its building management systems (Chapter 17);
- the general performance requirements and the product directions for the development of HVAC systems to better match the emerging needs of new ways of working (Chapter 18);
- the implications for the future directions of development of lighting systems (Chapter 19);
- the implications for future directions in the design of furniture and the layout of the office workplace (Chapter 20);
- the general trend of the development of information technology and its relationships to new ways of working (Chapter 21).

The previous evaluations of the separate affinities between the three major sets of variables (work patterns/building types; work patterns/HVAC systems; and building types/HVAC systems) are integrated into the summary tables that follow. Each table separately summarises the evaluations for each one of the four models of organisations:
- Hive
- Cell
- Den
- Club.

These tables therefore provide a means of focusing on which combinations of work pattern characteristics, building types and HVAC systems perform best, and which have particular problems, some of which may be amenable to improvement through new product development or design improvements.

Each table addresses the specific considerations of only one work pattern type, in relation to which each table identifies in a series of columns:
- the building type under consideration (*atrium, deep central core, medium depth, shallow depth*);
- the degree of affinity between the building type and the work pattern (good, adequate, or poor);
- the degree of affinity between the work pattern and one of four families of HVAC systems, (*distributed, all air, radiative air,* and *mixed mode*), under two different conditions of space layout: with low levels of enclosure or with high levels of enclosure ;
- the degree of affinity between the building type and the HVAC family system.

Moreover, using the cost model outlined earlier (Chapter 8), a summary of the expected costs of achieving a selection of the work pattern environments in some of the building types is also indicated, so that a basic measure of cost in relation to overall 'performance' is provided at the end of the section. This indicates the instances where a particular combination of work pattern, building type and HVAC system may perform very well but also cost more than other combinations. Note that the cost rating ••• equates to the lowest cost.

The tables are therefore a guide to thinking about how best to match work patterns to building types and to HVAC systems. They are not intended to be detailed guides to specification, or to prescribe particular solutions for individual organisations. Many individual building types and environmental systems can be tailored to suit most organisational requirements, the tables suggest on the basis of our research and evaluations what are nevertheless likely to be the best combinations of these critical elements, and which should be used as a starting point for the client/design team dialogue.

12.2 Hive

Building type	A. Work pattern: building type	B. Work pattern: HVAC	with low enclosure	with high enclosure	C. Building type: HVAC
 15M	•••	Distributed	••	n/a	••
		All air	••	n/a	•••
		Radiative air	•••	n/a	•••
		Mixed mode	•	n/a	•••
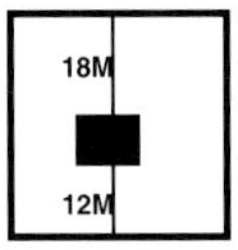 18M / 12M	•••	Distributed	••	n/a	•••
		All air	••	n/a	•••
		Radiative air	•••	n/a	•••
		Mixed mode	•	n/a	•••
 15M	•••	Distributed	••	n/a	•••
		All air	••	n/a	••
		Radiative air	•••	n/a	•••
		Mixed mode	•	n/a	•••
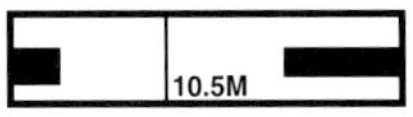 10.5M	•	Distributed	••	n/a	••
		All air	••	n/a	•
		Radiative air	•••	n/a	••
		Mixed mode	•	n/a	•••

Key:
••• good
•• adequate
• poor

Note: It is assumed that for the *hive* work pattern a highly enclosed space layout is inappropriate and unlikely.

Figure 54 Optimal affinities: the *hive* work pattern

12.3 Cell

Building type	A. Work pattern: building type	B. Work pattern: HVAC	with low enclosure	with high enclosure	C. Building type: HVAC
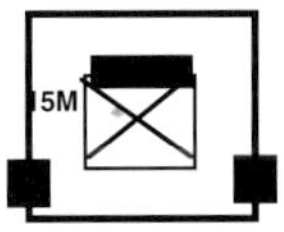	••	Distributed	••	••	••
		All air	••	••	•••
		Radiative air	•••	•(+•)[1]	•••
		Mixed mode	•	•••	•••
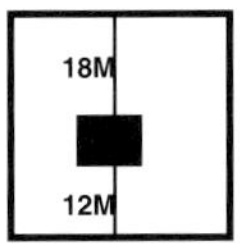	•	Distributed	••	••	•••
		All air	••	••	•••
		Radiative air	•••	•(+•)	•••
		Mixed mode	•	•••	•••
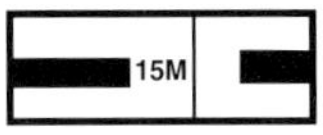	•••	Distributed	••	••	•••
		All air	••	••	••
		Radiative air	•••	•(+•)	•••
		Mixed mode	•	•••	•••
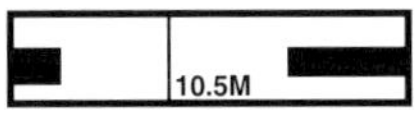	••	Distributed	••	••	••
		All air	••	••	•
		Radiative air	•••	•(+•)	••
		Mixed mode	•	•••	•••

Key:
- ••• good
- •• adequate
- • poor

[1] if improved local control and limited diversity

Figure 55 Optimal affinities: the *cell* work pattern

12.4 Den

Building type	A. Work pattern: building type	B. Work pattern: HVAC	with low enclosure	with high enclosure	C. Building type: HVAC
	•••	Distributed	•••	••	••
		All air	••	•••	•••
		Radiative air	•(+•)[2]	•	•••
		Mixed mode	•(+•)[3]	••	•••
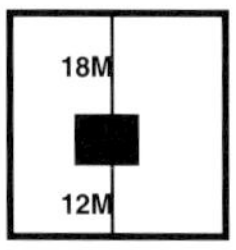	••	Distributed	•••	••	•••
		All air	••	•••	•••
		Radiative air	•(+•)	•	•••
		Mixed mode	•(+•)	••	•••
	•••	Distributed	•••	••	•••
		All air	••	•••	••
		Radiative air	•(+•)	•	•••
		Mixed mode	•(+•)	••	•••
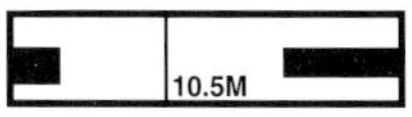	•	Distributed	•••	••	••
		All air	••	•••	•
		Radiative air	•(+•)	•	••
		Mixed mode	•(+•)	••	•••

Key:
- ••• good
- •• adequate
- • poor

[2] if static (ie not changing layout) the rating would be ••
[3] if high partitioning were installed the rating would be ••

Figure 56 Optimal affinities: the *den* work pattern

12.5 Club

Building type	A. Work pattern: building type	B. Work pattern: HVAC	with low enclosure	with high enclosure	C. Building type: HVAC
 5M	●●●	Distributed	●●●	●●	●●
		All air	●●	●●	●●●
		Radiative air	●	●	●●●
		Mixed mode	●	●●●	●●●
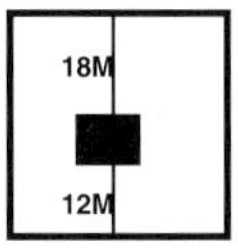 18M / 12M	●●●	Distributed	●●●	●●	●●●
		All air	●●	●●	●●●
		Radiative air	●	●	●●●
		Mixed mode	●	●●●	●●●
 15M	●●●	Distributed	●●●	●●	●●●
		All air	●●	●●	●●
		Radiative air	●	●	●●●
		Mixed mode	●	●●●	●●●
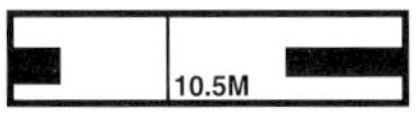 10.5M	●●●	Distributed	●●●	●●	●●
		All air	●●	●●	●
		Radiative air	●	●	●●
		Mixed mode	●	●●●	●●●

Key:
●●● good
●● adequate
● poor

Figure 57 Optimal affinities: the *club* work pattern

12.6 Integrating cost into performance evaluation

Hive

Building type	A. Work pattern: building type	B. Work pattern: HVAC	with Low enclosure	with high enclosure	C. Building type: HVAC	Cost rating
(building type 18M / 12M)	•••	Distributed	••	n/a	•••	•[4]
		All air	••	n/a	•••	••
		Radiative air	•••	n/a	•••	••
		Mixed mode	•	n/a	•••	•••

[4] the cost rating of the system is presented in terms of whether it is the same as the average (••) or at least 10% higher (•) or at least 10% lower (•••)

Figure 58 *Hive* work pattern in a *deep central core* building type, cost ratings of HVAC systems

- Independent of costs, within a *deep central core* building accommodating a *hive* organisation, the most effective HVAC system is *radiative air*.
- Independent of system types and their performance, within a *deep central core* building accommodating a *hive* organisation, the lowest cost HVAC system is *mixed mode*.
- Dependent upon all relationships, within a *deep central core* building accommodating a *hive* organisation, the *radiative air* HVAC system offers the highest ratings.

Building type	A: Work pattern: building type	B: Work pattern: HVAC	with low enclosure	with high enclosure	C. Building type: HVAC	Cost rating
(building type 15M)	•••	Distributed	••	n/a	•••	•
		All air	••	n/a	••	••
		Radiative air	•••	n/a	•••	••
		Mixed mode	•	n/a	•••	•••

Figure 59 *Hive* work pattern in a *medium depth* building type, cost ratings of HVAC systems

- Independent of costs, within a *medium depth* building accommodating a *hive* organisation, the most effective HVAC system is *radiative air*.
- Independent of system types and their performance, within a *medium depth* building accommodating a *hive* organisation, the lowest cost HVAC system is *mixed mode*.
- Dependent upon all relationships, within a *medium depth* building accommodating a *hive* organisation, the *radiative air* HVAC system offers the highest ratings.

Den

Building type	A. Work pattern: building type	B. Work pattern: HVAC	with low enclosure	with high enclosure	C. Building type: HVAC	Cost rating
[diagram 15M]	•••	Distributed	••	••	•••	•
		All air	••	•••	••	•
		Radiative air	•(+•)	•	•••	••
		Mixed mode	•(+•)	••	•••	•••

Figure 60 *Den* work pattern in *medium depth* building type, cost ratings of HVAC systems

- Independent of costs, within a *medium depth* building accommodating a *den* organisation, the most effective HVAC system is *distributed air.*
- Independent of system types and their performance, within a *medium depth* building accommodating a *den* organisation, the lowest cost HVAC system is *mixed mode.*
- Dependent upon all relationships, within a *medium depth* building accommodating a *den* organisation, the *distributed* and *mixed mode* HVAC systems offer the highest ratings.

Cell

Building Type	A. Work pattern: building type	B. Work pattern: HVAC	with Low enclosure	with High enclosure	C. Building type: HVAC	Cost Rating
[diagram 15M]	•••	Distributed	••	••	•••	•
		All air	••	••	••	•
		Radiative air	•••	•(+•)	•••	••
		Mixed mode	•	•••	•••	•••

Figure 61 *Cell* work pattern in *medium depth* building type, cost ratings of HVAC systems

- Independent of costs, within a *medium depth* building accommodating a *cell* organisation, the most effective HVAC systems are *distributed, radiative air* and *mixed mode.*
- Independent of system types and their performance, within a *medium depth* building accommodating a *cell* organisation, the lowest cost environmental (HVAC) system is the *mixed mode* system.
- Dependent upon all relationships, within a *medium depth* building accommodating a *cell* organisation, the *mixed mode* system offers the highest ratings.

Club

Building type	A. Work pattern: building type	B. Work pattern: HVAC	with low enclosure	with high enclosure	C. Building type: HVAC	Cost rating
	•••	Distributed	•••	••	••	•
		All air	••	••	•••	•
		Radiative air	•	•	•••	••
		Mixed mode	•	•••	•••	•••

Figure 62 *Club* work pattern in an *atrium* building type, cost ratings of HVAC systems

- Independent of costs, within an *atrium* building accommodating a *club* organisation, the most effective HVAC systems are *distributed*, *all air*, and *mixed mode*.
- Independent of system types and their performance, within an *atrium* building accommodating a *club* organisation, the lowest cost HVAC system is *mixed mode*.
- Dependent upon all relationships, within a *atrium* building accommodating a *club* organisation, the *mixed mode* system offers the highest ratings.

Club

Building type	A. Work pattern: building type	B. Work pattern: HVAC	with low enclosure	with high enclosure	C. Building type: HVAC	Cost rating
	•••	Distributed	•••	••	•••	•
		All air	••	••	•••	•
		Radiative air	•	•	•••	••
		Mixed mode	•	•••	•••	•••

Figure 63 *Club* work pattern in a *deep central core* building type, cost ratings of HVAC systems

- Independent of costs, within a *deep central core* building accommodating a *club* organisation, the most effective HVAC system is *distributed*.
- Independent of system types and their performance, within a *deep central core* building accommodating a *club* organisation, the lowest cost HVAC system is *mixed mode*.
- Dependent upon all relationships, within a *deep central core* building accommodating a *club* organisation, the *mixed mode* system offers the highest ratings.

Club

Building type	A. Work pattern: building type	B. Work pattern: HVAC	with low enclosure	with high enclosure	C. Building type: HVAC	Cost rating
		·Distributed	•••	••	•••	•
	•••	All air	••	••	••	•
		Radiative air	•	•	•••	••
		Mixed mode	•	•••	•••	•••

Figure 64 *Club* work pattern in a *medium depth* building type, cost rating of HVAC systems

● Independent of costs, within a *medium depth* building accommodating a *club* organisation, the most effective HVAC type is *distributed.*
● Independent of system types and their performance, within a *medium depth* building accommodating a *club* organisation, the lowest cost HVAC system is *mixed mode.*
● Dependent upon all relationships, within a *medium depth* building accommodating a *club* organisation, the *mixed mode* system offers the highest ratings.

13   The dynamics of change

Summary

From reviewing likely trends in organisational development (Chapter 13) and considering the transition that many organisations are likely to make particularly from *hive* and *cell* to *den* and *club*, we conclude that:

- the main, longer term trend in organisations is towards becoming more interactive and more intermittent in the use of time and space by individuals and groups;
- most larger organisations will continue to consist of a mix of the four organisational types: it is the proportion of each that will shift over time;
- the office building types that have the most capacity for accommodating this shift in organisational demand are the *medium depth atrium* and *medium depth* slabs;
- the families of HVAC systems that are most appropriate to facilitate this shift in organisational demand are likely to be more responsive and controllable at a local level than conventional *radiative air* or *all air* systems.

13.1 Accommodating dynamic organisations

The relationships between the organisation and building type, or between the environmental system and the organisation are never static. Neither can any one organisation be completely identified as either *club, den, hive* or *cell* in its work patterns and spatial characteristics. Reality, of course, is much more complex. Organisations are not only composed of varying proportions of types of patterns of work associated with particular groups, divisions or parts, but such combinations change over time. How are the results of this study likely to be affected by the fact that organisations are dynamic and change over time?

Our first underlying conclusion is that change is a constant condition of organisational existence. No single relationship between any building type or environmental system and any pattern of organisational requirements is likely to be sustained for very long. And yet buildings are likely to continue to be very long term entities and even environmental systems, although shorter in life span than buildings themselves, are certain to have to accommodate two, three or more generations of organisational structure.

Our second underlying conclusion is that the general directions of organisational change can be anticipated, even if the precise timetable of adoption of new organisational structures is very difficult, if not impossible, to determine. Taking a strategic view of the probable impact of external economic pressures and the internal momentum of the introduction of information technology into organisations, we predict that:

- much individual process work *(hive)* is likely to be exported to lower wage economies or to be automated;
- group process *(den)* and concentrated study *(cell)* are increasingly likely to merge or run parallel within increasingly plural work patterns;
- most office work will eventually tend to become transactional and *club*-like, with higher interaction and greater autonomy, for both individuals and groups;
- some work will become 'virtual', capable of being carried out in a totally aspatial way.

In other words we believe that the *hive, cell, den, club* model has an inherent dynamic trend towards greater interaction and more autonomy, ie a movement, more or less rapid, to the top right hand quadrant towards the office as *club*.

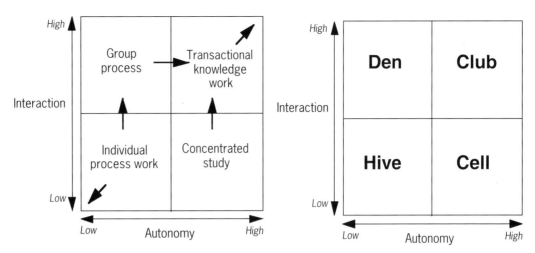

Figure 65 Directions for the future: accommodating change

13.2 Impact of these trends upon the models developed in the study

The key to optimising the future specification of new buildings is to understand the dynamics of organisational change and how this will relate to specification and building choices. Organisations will change the relative proportions of *hive, cell, den* and *club* type spaces they need. The total spectrum of organisational types will change its composition, with some types becoming more significant than others. To add to the complexity, the definitions of organisational types and their patterns of work will themselves evolve. Which building types, space layouts, products and environmental services are most likely to serve such organisational diversity and evolving demands?

The directions of movement are supported by the widespread emergence of new cultures of work. The common threads seem to be, compared to older organisational ways:

- much greater attention to the fluid and urgent use of time, ie the competitive advantage to be delivered from acting quickly and collectively;
- impatience with conventional organisational boundaries;
- not much love of hierarchies;
- a tendency towards smaller more transient organisational units, stripping the organisation back to the core, out-stripping redundant and non-central staff functions;
- the ability to provide the context and focus for intense, complex open ended teamwork;
- the obsolescence of clerks and clerical ways;

- greater reliance on the intelligent and creative use of Information Technology (IT);
- a wider range of types of work, settings for work, support for work, places for work.

Obviously, none of these emerging features of the new work cultures would be possible without powerful, integrated, interconnected and ubiquitous IT. It is, of course, IT with all its direct and indirect effects, which is enabling this series of managerial revolutions. It is IT which is dissolving conventions that have traditionally limited the use of time and place.

Den • more IT/intelligence • less stable boundaries • wider range of types of work, equipment	**Club** • virtual • multi-location • cross-corporate • replaced by city wide networks • shared consultants/others
Hive • automation • homeworking • work exported to 3rd world • more ergonomic choice	**Cell** • dispersed • homeworking • hotelling

Figure 66 Directions of change for organisational types

We can postulate in more detail how the individual patterns of work will evolve: not only will the relationships between the four work patterns change, some growing at the expense of others, others declining or disappearing, there will also be an evolution of the individual work patterns themselves. The types of organisations modelled will evolve, some, like the *club* will tend to increase in significance, others will decline or be exported, like the *hive*. The opportunities for remote working, telecommuting, and other impacts of technology will affect all organisational types. The *hive*, for example, seems likely to evolve into new forms, involving shift working and international networking for 24 hour world-wide services such as telesales or banking.

Will building types, differing significantly from those available today, be needed to accommodate these organisational developments more effectively and efficiently? We believe that it is not the basic building form that will have to be re-invented. Rather, given better means of servicing and managing office space more intelligently, a more limited array of basic office building forms is likely to be sufficient.

Club and *den* organisations can be accommodated in a wide range of building types characterised by basic variations of floor plan and configuration. Some smaller floor plate buildings will become more viable for larger scale organisations as the use of space is intensified over time. Both *very deep plan central core* buildings and *very shallow depth* buildings are likely to diminish in long term utility, but even they are capable of adaptive re-use. The implications for the design of buildings are further discussed in Chapter 17.

It is more important to ask which kind of environmental services can serve the changing requirements of workplaces demanded by the emergent organisational types? Which environmental services can most easily be adapted for change, added to and subtracted from in terms of capacity, quality of servicing, and subjected to different control strategies?

The key dynamics to consider are:
- the shift from *hive* to *den*, ie from low interaction to high interaction, autonomy remaining constant or increasing only slightly;
- the shift from *den* to *club*, ie from low to high autonomy; interaction being at a high level;
- the shift from *cell* to *club*, ie from low to high interaction, autonomy continuing at a high level.

Our findings suggest that as more organisations begin to work in new ways, the demands for *den* and *club* environments will increase. We believe this shift is best accommodated in the *medium depth* and *atrium* types of buildings. Environmental systems have not yet been fully developed to meet what we see as the expanding demands of the *den* and especially the *club* types of organisation. The *mixed mode* and *distributed* environmental systems seem most likely to have the capacity to be developed to match the demands of these more complex patterns of work and spatial layouts. The particular attributes of product directions needed to meet these demands are explored in Chapter 18.

13.3 Impacts of change on the development of HVAC systems

The dynamics of change in demand for HVAC systems are likely to involve several levels of development:
- the shift from one work pattern to another
- changes within work patterns themselves
- different combinations of work patterns.

Any of these changes could result in the need to:
- add to an HVAC system, for example to reduce zone sizes or extend the system to serve more rooms;
- reduce a system, for example to increase zone sizes or remove the system from a number of rooms;
- change spatial layouts that might affect air flow patterns (especially the installation or removal of partitions);
- change the densities and locations of occupancy thereby affecting air flow requirements;
- increase system capacity through upgrades of central plant, local units, or supplementary systems;
- increase the quality of servicing to become more responsive to new forms and levels of individual, or team, control;
- adapt the control strategy to serve extended occupancy as well as different kinds of occupancy;
- provide for multi-occupancy within a single building or floor, perhaps through one or multiple systems or by using the same delivery systems to offer warmth or cooling in different ways to different areas at different times.

There are a variety of issues which contribute to the ability of an HVAC system to be changed in these ways; including:

- ease of installation;
- ease of commissioning;
- ability to respond to changes in space layout;
- capacity to be upgraded;
- ability to be used in a *mixed mode* system.

The relative importance of each of these is dependent upon both the level of change being made within an organisation, and the building form. Changes could range from the addition of an extra fan coil terminal where the central plant margin is sufficient to avoid the need for any form of upgrade, to the installation of a complete comfort cooling or air conditioning system when a naturally ventilated building could no longer cope with the internal loads placed upon it.

The consultant survey undertaken as part of this study suggests the following simple ratings for 'designability' and 'integration' issues relating to the ability to cope with change of the different families of HVAC systems considered in this study. These evaluations are made independent of a consideration of the building type or work pattern. They therefore do not necessarily imply that the particular system family would be able to cope with the demands of the new work pattern.

HVAC system family	Ease of design	Ease of integration
All air systems	••	•
Tempered air	••	••
(Mixed mode is a combination of a tempered air system with a member of another system family)		
Distributed	••	••
Radiative air	•	••

Key:
•	poor
••	adequate
•••	good

Figure 67 Relative ease of design and ease of integration of HVAC systems. (Source: BRE survey of HVAC consultants, 1995.)

The management of change is further considered here in terms of differences in how the system families can maximise the usefulness of the HVAC services over the life time of the building when it is known what the changes in work patterns are likely to be. It is possible then to specify those system families which have a particular affinity for a given work pattern, and to consider this in relation to an allowance for moves from one work pattern to another.

The most important patterns of change are seen as being from *hive* to *cell*, from *cell* to *club* from *hive* to *den*, and from *den* to *club*. Within each of these it is possible to have either an enclosed or an open planned space layout, although the following table (Figure 68) confines itself to the most likely. The preferred HVAC system that would best support the shift from one work pattern to another is provided in italics.

The affinities of each family of HVAC systems for each work pattern have been explored in Chapter 10. In Figure 68 these assumptions of best affinity have been included. Note that it is possible for some individual HVAC system types to have particular characteristics that make them atypical relative to other HVAC types within the same family, especially under certain design or operating criteria. Moreover the table does not take into consideration the relationship of the HVAC system family to the building type (this has been explored in Chapter 11). The purpose of the table is to explore in a broad way the most likely possibilities associated with highest levels of affinity already developed in this study. The judgement of the design team and the client will of course remain essential in any real project.

From/To	Open cell	Enclosed cell	Open den	Enclosed den	Open club	Enclosed club
Open hive	Rad air[1]	Rad air - Mix mod[2]	Rad air - Dis or Rad air[3]	Rad air - All air[4]	Not applicable	Not applicable
Open cell	Not applicable	Not applicable	Not applicable	Not applicable	Rad air - Dis[5]	Rad air - Mix mod with All air or Dis [6]
Enclosed cell	Not applicable	Not applicable	Not applicable	Not applicable	Mix mod - Dis[7]	Mix mod - Mix mod with All air or Dis[8]
Open den	Not applicable	Not applicable	Not applicable	Not applicable	Dis - Dis[9]	Dis - Mix mod[10]
Enclosed den	Not applicable	Not applicable	Not applicable	Not applicable	All air - Dis[11]	All air - Mix mod[12]

Figure 68 Shifts in work patterns over time best supported by HVAC systems

[1] The natural choice for an open planned *hive* is a *radiative air* system. If this were to be converted into an open *cell* the *radiative air* system family would still be a possible choice. Although additional control is desirable in the cell this is difficult to provide in an open planned space very successfully. The *distributed* system would come closest with a possible move towards the personal desk ventilator (when proven) if user control was critical. However, a sophisticated *distributed* system is unnecessary for a *hive* environment.

[2] Moving from an open planned *hive* to an enclosed *cell* would infer changing from a *radiative air* system to a *mixed mode* system. The latter environment is chosen because of peoples' preference for natural ventilation and in an enclosed *cell* the high level of user control can be achieved by the provision of an openable window. Such a system would not be as suitable in an open planned *hive* due to the requirement for consistency and uniformity. It may be possible to install opening windows but to ensure that they remain locked, or have several opening elements so that for example just a top hopper can be opened, whilst the hive is in place. With care this may minimise the risk of draughts and conflict between those adjacent to, and far away from, windows. On moving to the enclosed *cell* it is possible to have the fully controllable windows provided that additional controls were put in place, for example high humidity lockouts to enable systems to act concurrently, as well as a sufficiently refined zoning of the *radiative air* system.

[3] The shift from an open planned *hive* to an open planned *den* involves moving from a *radiative air* to a *distributed* system. The *radiative air* system provides the consistency required by the *hive*, although if this were to be converted to a *den* some degree of zoning would need to be introduced to account for the different distribution of staff and to allow for an element of team control. This is feasible provided that the *dens* remain static. If a *distributed* system were installed attention would need to be paid to the location of terminal units so as to provide the facility for generating consistency of system control and to prevent certain staff from having a higher degree of system control than their colleagues, whilst the *hive* work pattern was in place.

[4] The shift from an open planned *hive* to an enclosed *den* would involve a move from a *radiative air* system to an *all air* system. The preferred option here is to begin with the *all air* system. This will provide the diversity required for dealing with the *den* and assuming that attention is paid to the flow paths and location of the terminals it will allow a fair degree of consistency for hive users. A variable flow system will allow energy savings to be made and would compensate for any slight differences across the space in terms of internal heat gain. If the *radiative air* system were used it would need to be extensively zoned.

[5] An open planned *cell* benefits most from a *radiative air* solution, whereas a conversion to an open *club* would ideally require a *distributed* system. Staff in an open *club* require a high level of individual control and loads can vary both across space and time on a more frequent basis than for other work patterns. The members of the *radiative air* family most able to offer a higher level of individual control in such an environment are the displacement ventilation with chilled beam options. However they do not rate very well against the requirements of the *club* due to their lesser ability to cope with the rapid variations and non-uniformity of this changing environment. An alternative would

be to begin with a member of the *distributed* family which offers the best solution for the open *club* and which still rates highly for the open *cell*. A further option may be to install an *all air* system which rates highly in both scenarios. The use of a well designed low temperature VAV system may offer the flexibility to cope with the diversity of loads associated with the *club* environment.

[6] The shift from an open planned *cell* to an enclosed *club* would mean a change from a *radiative air* to a *mixed mode* system. However a better solution may be to begin with an *all air* or *distributed* system which would perform equally well in both the *cell* and *club* situations. If a *mixed mode* system is chosen it may be preferable to look for a contingency system where the openable windows are not used until the building becomes an enclosed *club*. When the openable windows are to be used conflicts may arise with the *all air* or *distributed* system - a suitable control strategy would need to be implemented.

[7] The shift from an enclosed *cell* to an open planned *club* would appear to benefit most from a *distributed* system. Although not as desirable as the *mixed mode* would be for the enclosed *cell* initially, the *distributed* system still offers a high degree of user control and flexibility. The transition to an open planned *club* makes the *distributed* system even more attractive - as the *mixed mode* solution could lead to potential conflict with window opening.

[8] The shift from an enclosed *cell* to an enclosed *club* implies the installation of a mixed mode system from the outset. This could be either using an *all air* or a *distributed* system to allow for flexibility. Such a system may operate in a concurrent or changeover manner. A zoned system may pose problems with later changes to layout.

[9] The shift from an open planned *den* to an open planned *club* appears to favour the use of a *distributed* system which is rated very highly for both scenarios. A *distributed* system offers the best compromise between providing local control for teams (given that a consensus can be reached within the team) and satisfying diverse changing demands as called for by the *club*.

[10] The shift from an open planned *den* to an enclosed *club* could equally be achieved with a *distributed* system, with the possibility of a

mixed mode scenario if the open *den* were suitably partitioned to avoid conflict between team requirements and without affecting air flows.

[11] The shift from an enclosed *den* to an open planned *club* offers the option of choosing an *all air* system which best supports the enclosed *den* as it provides the requisite ability to deal with diversity and provide a reasonable level of local control for the team. Within the open *club* this system is not as versatile as a *distributed* system. An alternative may be to install the latter which would favour the *club* but which may be unnecessary for the expectations of the *den*.

[12] The shift from an enclosed *den* to an enclosed *club* has a variety of solutions. One possibility is the *all air* system with the same comments as previously. Another possibility, given the high degree of enclosure of both working patterns, is the use of a *mixed mode* system in conjunction with an *all air* system. The windows would add that extra degree of flexibility and user choice provided a suitable control strategy could be planned.

Part 4: Case studies

Part 1

Part 2

Part 3

Part 4

Part 5

Bibliography and appendices

The case studies of actual organisations in Europe and the USA are used to investigate the effectiveness of the models of work patterns, building types and environmental systems. The first set of case studies represent the variety of work patterns modelled: the *hive, cell, den* and *club*. They include:

- Automobile Association, Thatcham, England
- Andersen Consulting, Cleveland, USA
- Gasunie, Groningen, Netherlands
- Gruner + Jahr, Hamburg, Germany
- Lloyds Bank, Bristol, England
- Rijksgebouwendienst, Haarlem, Netherlands
- Sun Microsystems, Menlo Park, USA
- Walt Disney Imagineering, Burbank, USA

The particular ways of using space and the needs for environmental services of these organisations are explored. A second set of case studies investigates the ability of selected innovative servicing technologies to better meet the needs of organisations working in new ways. Evaluations of the relative performance of environmental systems and building types as found in the case studies provides directions for design improvements to building, space, and environmental systems and related products.

14 Organisations in Europe and the USA

Summary of findings

From a series of case studies chosen to illustrate a range of environmental systems in use by a cross-section of organisational types, we conclude that:

- the case study findings support the models of types of organisations and environmental systems developed in the research; however
- some organisations were succeeding in introducing innovative working practices and patterns of space and time use, despite apparently unsuitable buildings and environmental systems;
- other organisations were accommodated at great expense in buildings and environmental systems which in some respects were grossly over-designed;
- hence environmental systems cannot be properly evaluated for use by organisations without taking into account:
    - i)   how well they are integrated into the buildings that contain them;
    - ii) how they perform over time;
    - iii) how cost effective they are as capital expenditures and in use.

14.1 Learning from case studies

Two different kinds of case studies were undertaken. The first kind of case study focused on the experience of actual organisations, their work patterns, space use, and demands for environmental services. These cases were used to investigate the effectiveness of the models of work patterns, building types, and environmental system demands in the context of the actual experience of a set of organisations. The constraints and opportunities of the organisational demand and building supply model could be tested. Further implications for building and environmental system design to suit a range of organisational demands were identified.

The second set of case studies were technical in nature, reviewing and evaluating the performance of a range of innovative environmental systems.

Organisational case studies

The focus for the selection of organisations was that they should represent the range of work patterns modelled (*hive*, *cell*, *den*, and *club*). The organisations selected to be studied were:

Hive
- Automobile Association, Thatcham, England

Cell
- Andersen Consulting, Cleveland, Ohio, USA (shared bull pen settings)
- Gruner + Jahr, Hamburg, Germany (owned enclosed settings)

Den
- Gasunie, Groningen, Netherlands
- Lloyds Bank, Bristol, England
- Walt Disney Imagineering, Los Angeles, California

Club
- Rijksgebouwendienst, Haarlem, Netherlands
- Sun Microsystems, Palo Alto, USA.

A separate investigation was made of a so-called virtual organisation, the management consultancy in the UK called Change 2, to examine some issues of a spatial organisation that went beyond the scope of the methods of case studies used with the other organisations selected.

Technical case studies

A second set of case studies was selected to test the ability of a range of supposedly innovative servicing technologies to better meet the demands of new ways of working. It was intended that both of these kinds of case studies would help to identify issues that could be further explored for product development directions and design implications in the final phase of the research.

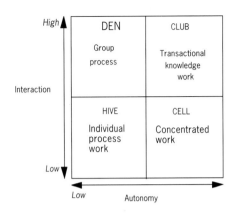

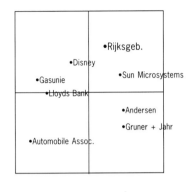

Figure 69 Positioning of organisational case studies

The other technologies and buildings studied were:
- Distributed system: Hiross flexible under-floor space system, at Eastern Group Headquarters, Ipswich, England
- Distributed system: ATM Zonal, at IBM UK, Bedfont Lakes, England
- Radiative air: Hollowcore, at Elizabeth Fry Building, UEA, Norwich, England
- Thorn Sensa overhead luminaires, Royal Bank of Scotland, London, England.

A separate literature based investigation was undertaken of personal desk ventilator systems, there being no suitable sites to examine in the UK.

Case study methods

A wide range of methods were used in the organisational case studies, including:
- gathering pre-visit information;
- a structured interview with a senior manager;
- a structured interview with a building or technical manager;
- a focus group discussion with building users;
- a micro observation study of the pattern of the use of space over time (wherever feasible);
- spot measurements of the internal environment;
- a survey of occupant satisfaction with the workplace;
- analysis and observation using plans, drawings and photographs.

The following section highlights some of the conclusions that were derived from the field work. A full report of detailed case study findings was provided to sponsors of the research. Only the most significant findings are reported here.

It is possible to relatively position in a relative way the organisational case studies using the framework which defines the organisational model described in Chapter 5, as shown in Figure 69. It should be noted that only those parts of the organisation that were studied in the case studies are positioned in the diagram. The diagram is not intended to represent the whole of the organisation. The positioning of these selected parts of the organisation is based partly on responses to interview questions, and by an assessment made by the project team.

The organisations represented a useful spread of different patterns of work achieved in a wide variety of workplaces and building types. They made use of many different kinds of environmental systems. For each of the case studies the project team evaluated in a simple way the degree of 'match' or appropriateness between the three critical relationships explored in the study:
- the work pattern: building type
- the work pattern: the HVAC system
- the building type: the HVAC system.

A summary of findings from each individual case study is provided in the following section, an overview of the findings is provided in Section 14.10.

14.2 Automobile Association

Call Handling Centre, Thatcham, England

Number of staff in case workplace	110
Type of project	Owner occupied, new build, designed 1988
Area	1,115 sqm gross, 948 sqm lettable
Organisational classification	Hive
Types of space	Large open plan space with associated support spaces
Typical working hours	24 hours, three staggered shifts of different sizes
Space ownership and management	Shared space for shift workers 24 hours
Building depth	17m glass to core
Density of space occupancy (people per/sqm lettable)	8.6 sqm effective; 50 people using the space on typical day
Type of environmental servicing	All air: constant volume, with natural ventilation in enclosed spaces with some fan coil units

Figure 70 Summary case study information

The organisation and its patterns of work

The Call Handling Centre is one of seven such centres distributed throughout the UK and Northern Ireland designed to receive, process and respond to calls from drivers seeking assistance. The location is driven by staffing requirements, ease of road access and parking. The Call Handling Centre receives calls from AA members within the region, these are taken by the call handlers. The call handlers deal with the public over the telephone and then process the relevant information on vehicle breakdowns and send it via the computer network for action by the deployment teams who communicate directly with the patrol fleet. The organisation operates 24 hours a day every day of the year. Shifts of both call handlers and deployment staff are used. The shifts are staggered across the day.

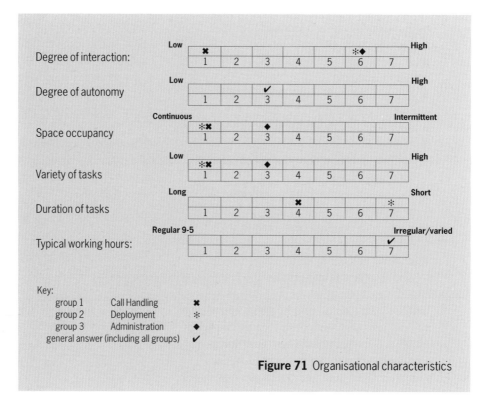

Figure 71 Organisational characteristics

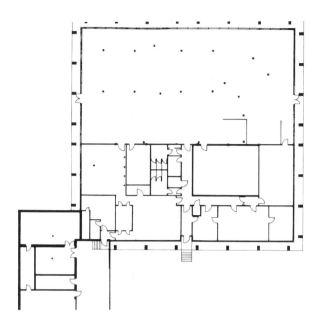

Figure 72 Base building plan

Figure 73 Exterior

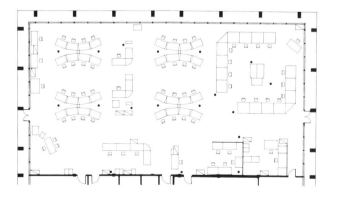

Figure 74 Layout

Figure 75 Interior

Environmental systems

Mostly sealed open plan space served by a constant volume variable temperature system with 'dx' coil and steam humidification. Heat recovery and free cooling are used when possible. Heating from compensated perimeter low temperature hot water finned convective strip and radiator system controlled with TRVs. Design specification is for 22+/-2°C in summer and 21+/-2°C in winter, with designed relative humidity of 50%. Lighting is provided by discharge up-lighters in the main working areas which are permanently on.

Evaluation

Simple and effective base building well suited to the *hive* work process. The HVAC systems occasionally find it difficult to cope with the demands of the work process for a consistent environment. Sometimes the air conditioning system in the open plan area is counteracted by opening doors to the outside air. There is a lack of system control for night shift working. The single zone provides insufficient control creating an unpredictable environment given the diversity of shift work loads imposed on the system. The match between the building type and the HVAC system is merely adequate. The lighting while not energy efficient is popular and has reduced glare problems.

14.3 Andersen Consulting

Cleveland, Ohio, USA

Number of staff in case workplace	205 using the 17th floor
Type of project	Fit out of leased space within older central core building (1959 building).
Area	One of three floors occupied, typical size is 1440 sqm
Organisational classification	Cell
Types of space	Mixed enclosed offices and shared open plan cubicle spaces
Typical working hours	Varied around core day depending on project deadlines, some weekends
Space ownership and management	Partners and associates in owned private offices; managers in shared 'Just-in-Time' offices (5:1); consultants and staff in shared open plan cubicles, (12:1); executive assistants in owned desks in open plan
Building depth, sectional height	13.2m glass to core, 3.96m floor to floor, 2.6m floor to ceiling
Density of space occupancy (people per/sqm lettable)	7.0 sqm effective with sharing; 24.8 sqm on space plan.
Type of environmental servicing	All air: constant volume, as well as distributed perimeter induction units

Figure 76 Summary case study information

The organisation and its patterns of work

Andersen Consulting offer management consulting services to corporate clients, their work is mostly based at the client's premises. Consultants come into the office to complete administrative, marketing and proposals work, communicate with secretaries and managers, and to undergo training. The organisation is structured through project teams within a career hierarchy. Teams are matrix skill based and based largely at the client's location, thus supporting the variety of ways in which space is shared over time within the office. Technology (Lotus Notes) is used extensively for intra company communication and shared tools. Secretarial and support staff are in the office full-time, while consultants are rarely in the office. The use of space is highly tailored to a hierarchy of patterns of occupancy: partners and associates in their own enclosed offices; managers usually share offices booked on a hotel reservation system ('Just-in-Time' officing) or have dedicated spaces depending on their need for privacy or on-site support (eg human resource personnel); consultants are in shared open plan cubicles used as needed.

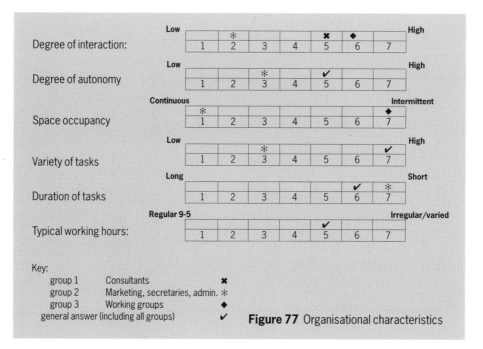

Figure 77 Organisational characteristics

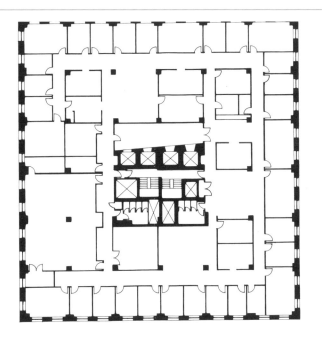

Figure 78 Base building plan

Figure 79 Exterior

Environmental systems

The mix of open and cellular spaces is served by a constant volume fixed temperature air conditioning system supplying and extracting via the ceiling, with two pipe induction units located beneath the windows. Units maintain extract air temperatures at between 21-23°C. Relative humidity is controlled to 50+/-10%. Air is re-circulated with a minimum of 15% fresh air. No user control is provided within the office areas. Lighting is fluorescent down lighters and task lighting switched on by occupants.

Evaluation

Andersen Consulting in Cleveland is looking for new premises believing that the building is no longer appropriate to their changing needs. The simple *central core* building, although old, provides good basic space for the work pattern of the organisation. The HVAC system offers high potential for localisation of control and system output but this has not been exploited or managed to match the demands of the organisation, the two systems remain separated. The HVAC system grid clashes with the space and furniture layout which in themselves do not well support the complex needs of the users in this advanced *cell* type of organisation.

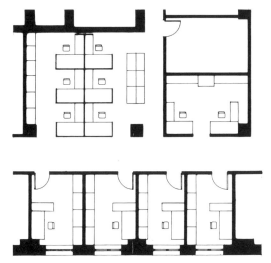

Figure 80 Layout

Figure 81 Interior

14.4 Gasunie

Headquarters, Groningen, Netherlands

Number of staff in case workplace	1,200
Type of project	New owner occupied building. Architect: Ton Alberts and Max van Hunt. Completed 1994
Area	45,000 sqm gross. 16 storeys
Organisational classification	DEN
Types of space	Combination of small group rooms (3 people) and individual enclosed offices
Typical working hours	Working days between 7.30 and 18.00, core between 9.00 and 16.30. Extended hours for computer centre and control room.
Space ownership and management	All individually owned settings except for 24 hour control centre
Building depth, sectional height	12.8 m glass to glass, 2.7 m floor to ceiling
Density of space occupancy (people per/sqm lettable)	Planned density is at 22.2 sqm per person, actual density is lower because not yet fully occupied
Type of environmental servicing	All air: VAV air conditioning in sealed building

Figure 82 Summary case study information

The organisation and its patterns of work

The gas utility headquarters is composed of many departments, the focus of the new building is to overcome differences within the organisation and improve communication. IT has been driving a high level of change. The organisation considers itself to be highly interactive, but this varies by groups. The high variety of work tasks and high rate of churn have been allowed for within a layout of small group rooms and individual offices all accessed from a central corridor across two wings. The skyscraper building form was intended to unite disparate departments around the vertical atrium serving the whole tower.

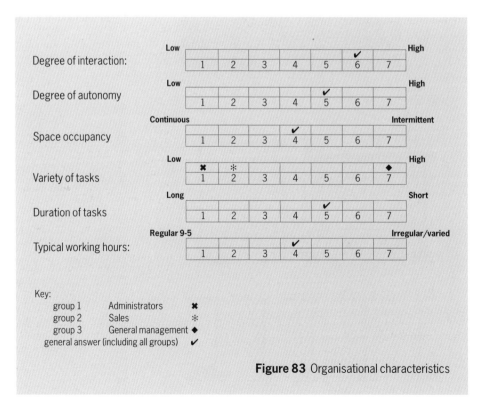

Figure 83 Organisational characteristics

Environmental systems

This sealed environment of cellular group rooms with some larger open group areas at the end of each wing is served by a variable volume air system with supply and extract via the ceiling, local control is provided within each room or area. Heating is provided by small perimeter radiators with electric heating in the open areas. Design temperatures are 23+/-2°C in summer and 21+/-2°C in winter with required relative humidities between 45-64%. General office lighting is high frequency fluorescent with local infrared user control.

Evaluation

The intended use of the building to promote communication between and among departments is frustrated by the restrictively shallow depth floors arranged on multiple storeys, as well as by the high levels of enclosure of the layout. The *den* style offices for three people provide neither for easy interaction across departments, groups or teams, nor for individual concentration. The attempt to provide for high levels of user control of the VAV system is frustrated by the control being room based rather than person based. There is potential conflict because the restricted layout of the furniture means staff have no option over where they sit. The HVAC controls are poorly understood. The lighting control could have been replaced by wall switches because it only provides shared control anyway. An expensive and high image building that does not meet its true potential.

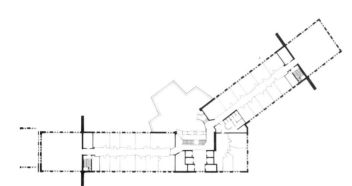

Figure 84 Base building plan

Figure 85 Exterior

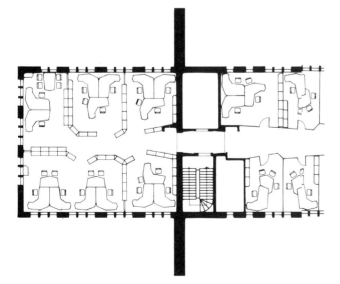

Figure 86 Layout

Figure 87 Interior

14.5 Gruner + Jahr

Druck-und Verlagshaus, Hamburg, Germany

Number of staff in case workplace	2,000
Type of project	New build owner occupied. Architect: Stedle & Partner, Kissler & Partner. Completed and occupied 1990
Area	60,000 sqm
Organisational classification	Cell
Types of space	Highly cellular enclosed rooms in most areas
Typical working hours	9.00-17.00, but varies by department and deadlines
Space ownership and management	Owned individual settings
Building depth, sectional height	13m glass to glass, 2.75m floor to ceiling, 3.5m floor to floor
Density of space occupancy (people per/sqm lettable)	Approximately 30 sqm per person
Type of environmental servicing	Mixed mode: VAV air conditioning with natural ventilation, opening windows

Figure 88 Summary case study information

The organisation and its patterns of work

Headquarters for the largest magazine publisher in Germany, composed of many sub-organisations focused around individual magazine titles all served by central advertising, distribution, archive and library services. The focus of work is the individual editorial process, creative and highly autonomous tasks. The high value placed on individual responsibility is balanced by the recognition of the importance also of team work on the magazines. The offices are designed as individual cells to provide for very high levels of individual control over the workplace environment. Generous circulation routes and streets are intended to foster interaction among individuals. Even though individual office space is the norm, the architect intended the building to be transparent and to support communication.

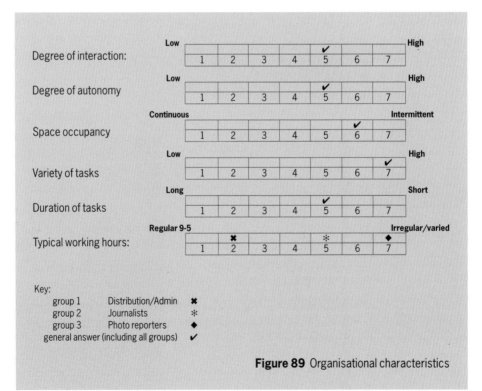

Figure 89 Organisational characteristics

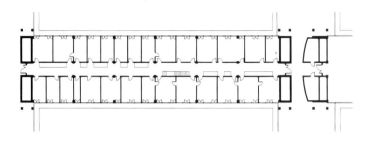

Figure 90 Base building plan

Figure 91 Exterior

Figure 92 Layout

Environmental systems

The cellular offices on the upper floors are served by both opening windows and a variable air volume (VAV) system which supplies air through grilles in the floor and extracts through high level wall grilles. The VAV system can be controlled by wall switches in each office which enables it to be switched on if the external conditions rise above 23°C in the summer or when they fall to 10°C, and if the relative humidity falls outside of acceptable limits. There are no window switches to prevent occupants using the AC whilst their windows are open. Heating is by TRV-controlled finned skirting hot water radiators. Lighting is a combination of overhead and task lighting.

Evaluation

The shallow depth of the typical office floors and the over reliance on individual enclosed office rooms restricts the capacity of the base building to provide for larger scale project, group, or team interaction within and between departments. Nevertheless, the sophisticated and expensive HVAC systems provide highly advanced capacity for individual control and quality in the offices which they make appropriate use of despite the lack of interlock between the windows and the AC system. The task lighting is well used and energy efficient. In some respects the systems are over-specified, with areas of over provision of servicing and control elements that tend to conflict with each other and with the design features of the building, especially its very high levels of glazing.

Figure 93 Interior

14.6   Lloyds Bank

Headquarters for retail banking, Bristol, England

Number of staff in case workplace	1,400
Type of project	New build owner occupied. Architect: Arup Associates
Area	16,590 sqm lettable (Phases 1 and 2)
Organisational classification	Den in most areas
Types of space	All open plan
Typical working hours	Core day 9.00-17.00 but flexible between 7.30 and 19.30
Space ownership and management	All individually owned desks
Building depth, sectional height	Either 18m glass to glass (Phase 2) or 12m glass to atrium (Phase 1) 4.05 floor to floor; floor to underside of beam is 2.55m (600mm access floor for cables and AC)
Density of space occupancy (people per sqm lettable)	11.8
Type of environmental servicing	All air: under-floor constant volume air conditioning with perimeter distributed four-pipe fan coils

Figure 94 Summary case study information

The organisation and its patterns of work

The head office for retail banking operations in the UK involves many different departmental functions, ranging between a minority of desk bound *hive* types of work such as the telephone help lines, to more common interactive groups and teams working in the large scale open planned areas. Three basic types of work occur: direct customer interactions; distribution of information and services to the retail operations; and infrastructure support for the whole organisation, for example in property services. The work processes vary between groups, but a predominant pattern is that of the *den*: high levels of group interaction with varied levels of individual autonomy. Lower autonomy work is associated with the bank's need to maintain reliability and consistency in the financial processes, yet the organisation is seeking to encourage more individual and group empowerment and initiative at all levels. The new building was intended to support the change away from a largely enclosed, isolated and hierarchical use of space in dispersed office buildings towards an open work environment encouraging inter-dependence, change and communication.

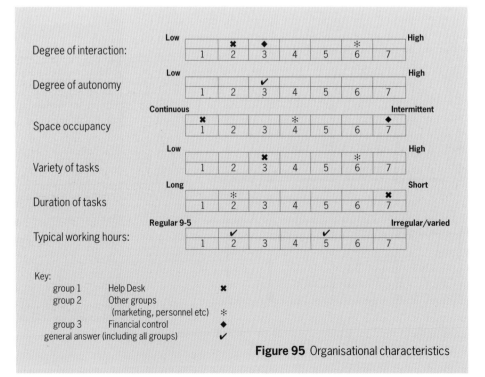

Figure 95 Organisational characteristics

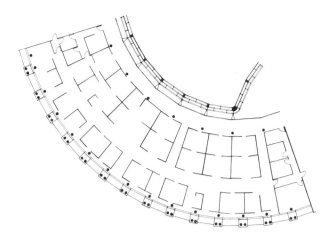

Figure 96 Base building plan

Environmental systems

A constant volume system serves the open plan offices supplying cooled air to a sealed floor plenum with small floor grilles. Air is supplied at a constant 20°C to maintain internal conditions at 21+/-2°C. Humidity is controlled between 40-50% when possible although dehumidification is unavailable. Under-floor four-pipe fan coils provide additional cooling at the outer perimeter. Local dock water is used as coolant. Exhaust air is returned through the light fittings and ducted through to the slab in the floor, eliminating the need for a ceiling void. No task lighting is provided, although there is control over banks of lighting via wall mounted switches.

Evaluation

A simple set of space standards has allowed a wide variety of groups to establish their needs and work together in different ways, even though the open plan layout restricts the degree of user control that it is possible to provide. *Den* type layouts are created by using different heights of screens and selecting furniture as a kit of parts to suit group or individual requirements. The *den* style of layout supports a consensus approach to control of systems, supporting the use of the under-floor *all air* systems with additional distributed services in key areas. A more group oriented approach to the control of systems might be beneficial, as would a finer resolution to the light switching combined with task lighting. Overall the performance of the building and its HVAC systems work well for the organisation, although the HVAC system is in some ways over-specified for the requirements.

Figure 97 Exterior

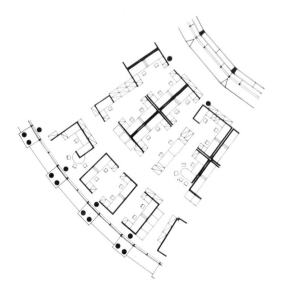

Figure 98 Layout

Figure 99 Interior

14.7   Rijksgebouwendienst

Directie Nord East, Haarlem, Netherlands

Number of staff in case workplace	23
Type of project	Refurbished leasehold within an existing 1980s office building. Furniture design by Gispen. Prototype office
Area	199 sqm lettable in pilot area
Organisational classification	Club
Types of space	Mixture of open and enclosed work areas with associated support spaces
Typical working hours	Flexible time between 7.30 to 18.00, typically 8 or 9 hours
Space ownership and management	Mixture of shared spaces (small glazed enclosures) for nomadic area managers, and other open group or cell spaces for staff permanently in the office
Building depth	18m glass to glass
Density of space occupancy (people per sqm lettable)	8.6 sqm effective with sharing
Type of environmental servicing	Mixed mode: VAV air conditioning and opening windows for perimeter natural ventilation

Figure 100 Summary case study information

The organisation and its patterns of work

This regional office for property managers who are often out of the office allows for shared space use by the managers. The refurbished *club* type space is driven by a new organisational concept to promote more interaction and communication among staff as well as to minimise environmental impacts by reducing space and services demand per person. Very small glazed cells (2m x 1.7m) are shared, while a group room for support staff and two dedicated enclosed offices areas are used by other financial staff. A wide variety of informal meeting areas and enclosed meeting spaces are also provided along with grouped central filing systems and mobile pedestals.

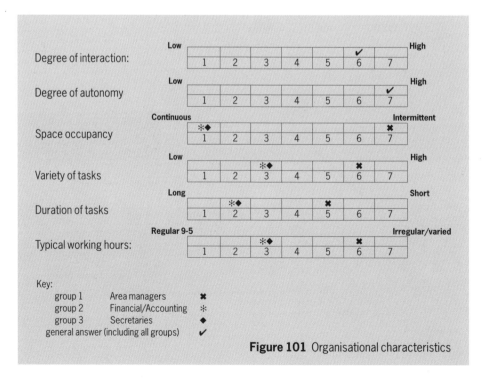

Figure 101 Organisational characteristics

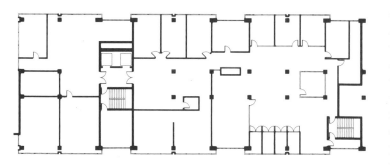

Figure 102 Base building plan

Environmental systems

The combination of small enclosed perimeter offices and interior open spaces is served by opening windows and a variable air volume system with fan assisted terminals. In winter the air to the VAV system is heated and in summer it is pre-cooled when the external temperature rises above 21°C. At other times cooling is achieved by altering the air supply rate. Supply and extract are through the ceiling. Supplementary heating is provided at the perimeter by low temperature hot water convectors. There is no interlock between the windows opening and the VAV system. High levels of user control for this *club* type of organisation are provided, but without tight design conditions. Photocell controlled lighting is being tested, all other lights have pull cords or wall switches.

Evaluation

This advanced *club* office, optimising a wide range of work settings and their pattern of use to match the work process, works very well. The HVAC systems, however, are unable to perform well within the refurbished building to suit these complex demands. Conflicts between window opening and blind operation are reinforced by the mismatch between building grid and the very small new office modules. The air distribution system has not been re-balanced to service varied room sizes and the erratic patterns of use. Preferred areas have arisen due to inconsistency of achieved conditions. Control interface is not intuitive as the dials relate to air flow rather than temperature. Furnishing and layout are the critical elements of success here.

Figure 103 Exterior

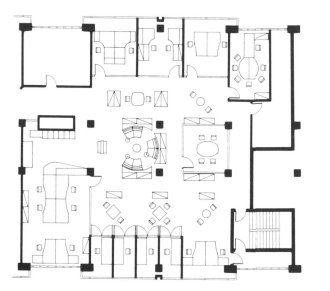

Figure 104 Layout

Figure 105 Interior

14.8 Sun Microsystems

MARCOM group, Menlo Park, Palo Alto, California, USA

Number of staff in case workplace	46 in the Marketing and Communications group (Marcom)
Type of project	Campus of developer speculative buildings, fitted out for Sun. Architect: Backen Arrigoni Ross. Interiors by Bottom Duvivier, 1995.
Area	1858 sqm occupied by the Marcom group. Typical building floors are 4,600–5,100 sqm
Organisational classification	Club and cell
Types of space	Mixture of individually owned cells alongside shared interactive project spaces
Typical working hours	Varied with project deadlines around core times
Space ownership and management	Individual enclosed offices (fully glazed in Marcom) with shared team areas
Building depth	14.4m from glass to core, 37m glass to glass in the Marcom area
Density of space occupancy (people per sqm lettable)	24 sqm
Type of environmental servicing	All air: variable air volume air conditioning with heat only perimeter fan coils

Figure 106 Summary case study information

The organisation and its patterns of work

The Menlo Park campus at Palo Alto is the headquarters of the Sun Microsystems Computer Corporation, the main division responsible for hardware. The work culture is highly task oriented. Hardware and software specialists need access to excellent technology using individual offices, laboratories and a range of team facilities. The Marketing and Communications group involves multi-skilled teams including artwork and graphics to produce external communications. Their space provides for focused individual work in small glazed cubicles (2.4m x 3.6m) adjacent to interactive team areas. The team areas are designed with highly flexible project furniture and systems for use with IT as well as display facilities.

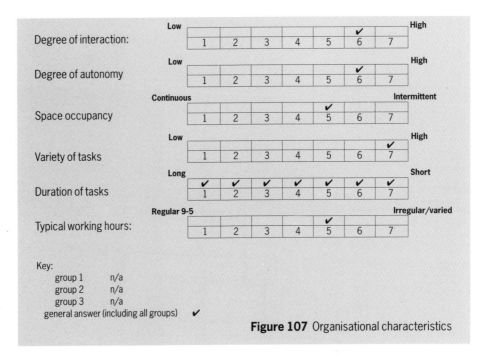

Figure 107 Organisational characteristics

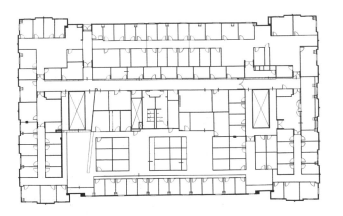

Figure 108 Base building plan

Environmental systems

The deep planned cellular space is served by a variable air volume system linked to heat only fan coils at the perimeter zone. Air is supplied and extracted through the ceiling plenum. Each VAV terminal supplies six cellular offices and no user control is provided. The design is for 24+/-1°C with no humidity control. Lighting is provided by up-lighters to reduce glare, combined with task lighting. The BMS controls the lighting and small power provision to occupancy sensing.

Evaluation

The simple deep developer buildings have allowed Sun to achieve a highly collaborative group environment which also permits concentrated individual work. Furniture and lighting systems are highly controllable and effective. The HVAC systems using a sophisticated central BMS will be effective so long as staff become familiar with how to use it. We would expect this kind of quasi-*club* environment to provide a higher degree of user control. The lack of individual control of HVAC is compensated for by highly functional lighting and small power controls, factors that work well with the highly intensive IT focus of the work pattern. Other specialised areas of the office are served by separate systems, this may mitigate against the frequent re-organisation of space and interiors expected in a *club* type of organisation.

Figure 109 Exterior

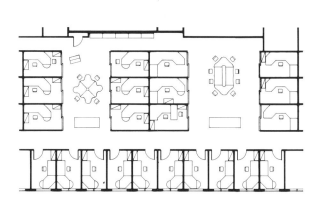

Figure 110 Layout

Figure 111 Interior

14.9   Walt Disney Imagineering

Mapo building, Burbank, California, USA

Number of staff in case workplace	1,200 total of which 100 in Florida and 150 elsewhere in Los Angeles. 150 in the MAPO building
Type of project	Refurbished leased old industrial space
Area	6,875 sqm gross, of which 4422 sqm is office space.
Organisational classification	Den
Types of space	Mixture of cellular and project team areas as well as large display areas
Typical working hours	7-8.00 – 17.00-19.00, flexible hours.
Space ownership and management	Owned individual settings with shared project team spaces and other support space
Building depth	36.4m glass to glass
Density of space occupancy (people per sqm lettable)	Approximately 24.7 sqm in the office/project areas
Type of environmental servicing	All air: VAV air conditioning

Figure 112 Summary case study information

The organisation and its patterns of work

Walt Disney Imagineering is the organisational brain behind the Disney theme parks, the home of the famous 'Imagineers'. It is the master planning and brainstorming centre for the creative development, design, engineering, production and project management for the theme parks. The organisation depends on 'corridor culture' and the use of so-called 'skunk teams' of specialist problem solvers using mixed skills brought together to focus on projects. 25 senior managers work with 110 designers and 15 support staff. The circular project process relies on a sequence of individual and group work with constant review and links to other teams. Display space for project teams is an essential feature of the workplace and serves to keep the whole organisation informed. Core employees are supported by many out-sourced workers.

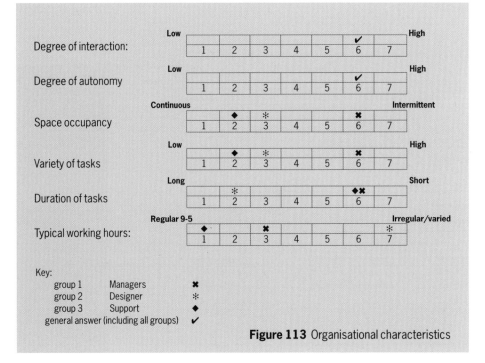

Figure 113 Organisational characteristics

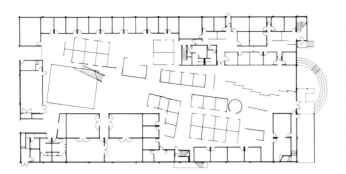

Figure 114 Base building plan

Figure 115 Layout

Environmental systems

This *den* organisation is planned in spaces where each individual and group is highly screened. Servicing is provided by a variable air volume system with each zone having its own packaged unit. Zoning is inherited and does not necessarily match the actual requirements. Supply and extract in the office areas is via the ceiling with temperatures controlled between 23-25°C, with no humidity control. Wherever possible pre-emptive actions such as pre-cooling are taken if very diverse loads are anticipated. Lighting is fluorescent down lighting controlled by wall switches.

Evaluation

The large volumes of space in the industrial building allow for the mixture of individual cell spaces and large scale project team and display areas. However, many staff are remote from daylight in the very deep spaces. Problems have arisen with the match between the zoning and later office re-configurations. The HVAC system does not work well in the large space volumes, *radiative* systems combined with airborne conditioning in office spaces would be a better solution. The systems were further compromised by the poor location and explanation of controls. User control of the HVAC systems is possible via LAN access to the BMS but this is not encouraged because of potential conflict with neighbouring staff. The aim is to support the team environment, with only lighting under individual control.

14.10 Summary case study evaluations

The project team evaluated the case studies in order to understand their implications for potential improvements to building, space, and environmental services design and related products. This provided directions for the further work on technical case studies that took place after the organisational studies were completed. The project team evaluations of each case study examined:

- the base building types and the generic environmental servicing types
- space layout and scenery and the installed environmental services
- an estimate of total quality overall of both building/layout and generic/installed environmental services systems
- an estimate of the normalised effective cost of the achieved building/environment and an estimate of the total effectiveness of the achieved building and its environmental services.

The evaluations represented the project team's assessment of the key variables analysed in the case studies in order to understand the problems of relative performance and effectiveness. They alerted the project team to the need to consider the relative effectiveness of building types and environmental systems in a context of both different levels of expectation and specification associated with

organisational types or patterns of work (*hive, cell, den* and *club*) and their associated levels of cost. This led directly to instigation of work with Johnson Controls Limited on developing a preliminary cost model linked to the organisational types. Some of the comments associated with the evaluations are reproduced below to indicate how the team developed its thinking in this area.

Base building type: generic environmental services systems

- Automobile Association has a good simple base building, but this was not quite as well matched by the quality of specification of the environmental services.
- Gasunie is accommodated in a high image and high cost building that is somewhat inflexible and inappropriate for the user requirements, although the environmental servicing systems would appear to be appropriate.
- Gruner + Jahr is a very high performance serviced environment within a building type that is not completely successful (and achieved at high cost).

The evaluations highlight the problem of balancing the performance of the base building type with the generic environmental servicing system, as well as the need to evaluate both against the cost of the achievement in relation to organisational requirements and levels of expectation.

Issue	Automobile Association	Gruner + Jahr	Andersen Consulting	Lloyds Bank	Gasunie	Walt Disney Imagineering	Sun Micro Systems	Rijksgebouw- endienst
Work pattern	Hive	Cell	Cell	Den	Den	Den	Club	Club
Activity	Call handling centre	Creative office for writers and editors	Mgmnt. consulting	Retail banking HQ	Gas utility HQ	Concept design and development	Marketing and comms	Property management
Time and space use	24 hour shift work	Variable use of individual enclosed offices	Shared 'Just in Time' open plan and cell space	Groups and depts. in open plan, regular day	Very small groups in group offices, regular day	Studio based group areas, varied use for team projects	Individual small cells with shared team spaces, flexible time use	Variety of shared and owned settings used as needed

Figure 116 Summary descriptions of organisational case studies

Issue	Automobile Association	Gruner+ Jahr	Andersen Consulting	Lloyds Bank	Gasunie	Walt Disney Imagineering	Sun Micro Systems	Rijksgebouw-endienst
HVAC system	All Air CV in open plan	Mixed Mode Nat vent. + VAV	All air/ Distributed	Distributed four-pipe fan coil	All air VAV + atria	All air VAV	All air/ Distributed VAV + Fan coil	Mixed mode VAV + nat. vent.
Base building type						Deep warehouse	Extra-deep	Old
Building type: work pattern	•••	••	•••	•••	•	••	•••	••
Work pattern: HVAC	•	•••	••	•••	••	••	••	••
Building type: Environmental system	••	•••	•••	•••	•	••	••	••
Remarks	Good simple building, poor services design	High cost highly specified services; building is too shallow	Simple base building but not very good servicing	Well matched base building and services	High cost and not highly effective base building	Poor quality base building and services	Very deep *atrium* building suits project work	Old refurbished base building difficult to match *club* demands

Key:
••• good
•• adequate
• poor

Figure 117 Summary of evaluations of organisational case studies

Appropriateness of space layout and scenery and the quality of installed environmental systems

- Rijksgebouwendienst achieved very high quality of layout, scenery, and interior design to support the *club* office users but within an older refurbished building that could not provide a corresponding quality of installed environmental services
- Andersen Consulting represented a relative under-performance of the installed environmental services system in relation to the capacity of the generic environmental services system
- Gruner + Jahr achieved very high quality environmental servicing but within a space layout that is not highly effective for the organisation given their need to balance individual concentration work with team interaction

The overall summary achievement scores highlighted the necessity of evaluations to incorporate cost in relation to performance. This would, for example, have enabled the Rijksgebouwendienst to have achieved a higher evaluation to better represent their cost effective and high quality workplace.

In addition, the evaluations need to better account for the relative variations of expectation and specification associated with *hive, cell, den* and *club* types of environments, so that, for example, the cost/performance evaluation of the Automobile Association's *hive* office would be targeted differently to that of a *club* style environment.

If cost and performance are to be evaluated in relation to the expectations of the user types, then the two overall 'top' achievers in this evaluation are the *club* environment at Rijksgebouwendienst and the simple *hive* environment at the Automobile Association.

15 Case studies of technologies

15.1 Elizabeth Fry Building, University of East Anglia, Norwich, England

The organisation and its work patterns

The Elizabeth Fry Building is one of a number of combined office and teaching centres on the University of East Anglia (UEA)campus on the western side of Norwich. The building provides cellular office accommodation for the academic staff of the School of Social Work but also provides overspill accommodation for other University departments.

	Percentage dissatisfaction			
	0-25%	26-50%	51-75%	76-100%
Winter-time temperature	21%			
Summer-time temperature	17%			
Winter-time air movement	12%			
Summer-time air movement	17%			
Control over temperature				79%
Control over ventilation			60%	
Control over lighting		28%		

	0-25%	21-40%	41-60%	61-80%	81-100%
Overall dissatisfaction with building	9%				

Figure 118 User satisfaction with environmental systems

The lecture theatres and seminar rooms are used intensively as they are available to all the University departments. The office accommodation has quite a variable occupancy due to the nomadic nature of the academic staff. Also, many staff spend much of their non-teaching time working from home, using their office as a base whilst at the University and as a storage location for the large quantities of literature required for their research activities. However, some staff members prefer to work from their office and, due to the variable nature of combined research and teaching duties, often work until 10 or 11pm.

Environmental systems

The building environment is controlled by a Termodeck hollow core ventilation system. This maximises the interaction of the 100% fresh air supply with the building fabric, so as to achieve maximum thermal storage, and hence dampen the diurnal swings in internal temperature, minimising the need for mechanical heating and cooling.

The core ends of each ceiling/floor slab are blocked and interconnecting holes cut to create an extended air pathway within the slab. Air is drawn through the slabs at low speed by a fan so as to maximise the heat transfer between the air and the concrete whilst avoiding excessively turbulent flow induced by the rough surface of the concrete walls of the cores at high flow rates.

Winter operation of the Termodeck system involves pre-heating the 100% fresh air through a heat recovery unit and re-heating (if required) to about 35°C. This heated air is passed through the concrete slabs where 70° of its heat is stored for dissipation during the following night. The fresh air and the remaining heat is delivered to the space below through ceiling diffusers. During unoccupied periods the fans are normally off unless additional 'top-up' heating is required, when the system operates on 100% recirculation.

Summertime operation involves the passing of filtered but untreated 100% fresh air through the slab at night to cool it using the natural overnight drop in temperature. During the daytime, fresh air is again passed through the slab, cooled by contact with the pre-cooled slab and hence holding down the temperature of the air entering the space to approaching that of the slab temperature.

Evaluation of environmental systems

The Termodeck system in highly insulated, thermally heavy buildings operates a passive cooling system for the majority of the year. The high thermal capacity absorbs both intermittent and constant internal heat loads over the occupied period whilst maintaining stable diurnal Dry Resultant Temperature. Conditioning the whole building with constant air flow rates and low fan powers allows simple controls to be used. Variable occupancy rooms (eg lecture theatres) can use either CO_2-controlled variable speed fans or manually controlled switch flow operation matching both ventilation and cooling loads to the internal requirements.

The Elizabeth Fry building includes openable windows which provide the occupants with the user control they lack with the Termodeck system. This *mixed mode* combination, although inefficient as the air supply through the *all air* Termodeck cannot be turned off when the windows are open, appears to work well in this closed cellular environment. The *radiative air* nature of the system means the loss of air through open windows is less energy wasteful than would be the case with a convection based heating/cooling system.

The occupants have been educated to shut the windows once the temperature outside is greater than that inside in order to maximise the benefit of the Termodeck cooling capacity. Despite the inefficiencies within the Termodeck system, the Elizabeth Fry building is a low energy solution to the treatment of a building of this nature.

15.2 IBM UK,
Bedfont Lakes, Heathrow, England

The organisation and its work patterns

2 New Square is one of three buildings occupied by IBM UK on the Bedfont Lakes office park. The three-storey building houses the national marketing centre as well as being the main UK customer centre, where IBM customers visiting the centre are encouraged to make use of the facilities for their own business needs. The majority of the predominantly open plan office space is around the perimeter of the first and second floors, with open spaces on the ground floor of the large central atrium providing communal dining facilities and display areas.

	Percentage dissatisfaction			
	0-25%	26-50%	51-75%	76-100%
Winter-time temperature	25%			
Summer-time temperature	10%			
Winter-time air movement	25%			
Summer-time air movement	20%			
Control over temperature			75%	
Control over ventilation				83%
Control over lighting		40%		

	0-25%	21-40%	41-60%	61-80%	81-100%
Overall dissatisfaction with building		27%			

Figure 119 User satisfaction with environmental systems

The building occupancy is quite variable, being the base for approximately 1000 IBM staff of which many are mobile sales staff. Some of the staff operate a hot-desking scheme whilst others work a more standard 9 to 5 non-desk-sharing work pattern. Although many of the staff work in teams some of these tend to be quite fluid and short lived as is often the case for a *club* environment.

Environmental systems

The internal environment of the office spaces is controlled by a zoned air treatment module (ATM) system whilst the atrium is conditioned with re-circulated air from the office spaces. A separate variable air volume (VAV) system is used to treat the conference areas. The ATM units are fan coils located outside the occupied space in small on-floor plant rooms. Tempered air is distributed to the plant rooms by roof-top central plant, where it is heated or cooled as required by the ATM units before being distributed to the occupied space by means of flexible ducts. The modular nature of the ATM system allows each unit to be controlled individually or as part of a zoned control, as well as enabling the rapid removal of a unit for maintenance.

Evaluation of environmental systems

The system is designed to minimise the maintenance which is carried out in the occupied space. As such it is particularly applicable to buildings with long occupied periods where out of hours maintenance can be a problem. An additional benefit is that wet services are not transported through the ceiling voids of the occupied space, reducing the risk of water damage to IT equipment, etc. The modularity of the system combined with centrally programmable local controllers enables rapid reconfiguration of the system providing the flexibility to respond to high levels of churn. Within an open *club* environment a *distributed* system is a good choice in terms of providing user control.

However, the high level of user control offered by the ATM system, by allowing occupants to control each of the ATM units individually, was not implemented in this building because of concerns that the open plan nature of the accommodation would cause inefficient simultaneous heating and cooling in adjacent spaces. Instead, the ATMs are controlled on a zonal basis by the central BMS. Individual control is provided in a few of the cellular managers' offices. Although maintenance is made more convenient than for many other systems, there is a need to consider a suitable maintenance regime for the very large numbers of ATM units.

Technology
Case Study 3

15.3 Eastern Electricity Group Headquarters
Ipswich, England

The organisation and its work patterns
The Eastern Electricity Group headquarters are located on the outskirts of Ipswich in the Wherstead Park Estate House which was converted for this purpose. The area considered in this study is the first and second floors of an extension built onto the front of the original main building. Both floors are predominantly open plan with a small number of cellular offices and meeting rooms on the internal perimeter.

	Percentage dissatisfaction			
	0-25%	26-50%	51-75%	76-100%
Winter-time temperature	8%			
Summer-time temperature	11%			
Winter-time air movement	25%			
Summer-time air movement	17%			
Control over temperature				85%
Control over ventilation				83%
Control over lighting				94%

	0-25%	21-40%	41-60%	61-80%	81-100%
Overall dissatisfaction with building		34%			

Figure 120 User satisfaction with environmental systems

The offices have an external view on their western facade and look into a glazed courtyard, now forming an atrium, on their eastern side. The design occupancy is one person per 10 sqm which corresponds in theory to about 50 people per floor although in practice the occupancy is unbalanced with the first floor housing about 65 staff. The building operates as an open plan cellular arrangement. Although people tend to be arranged in teams they operate mostly as individuals carrying a high level of responsibility for what they do and with the expectations of being able to control their working environment accordingly.

Environmental systems
The two floors studied are served by a Hiross Flexible Space System using a modular raised floor to deliver air conditioning and for electrical and communications cabling. Although it is then possible through the use of up-lighters to eliminate the need for a false ceiling, as this is a refurbishment project the original ceiling and down-lighting has been kept. The air is treated by a number of CAM units located in cupboards within the space. Each one can serve an area of approximately 300 sqm. The CAM unit receives fresh air treated by a central air handling unit and re-circulated air from the floor void. It filters, heats/cools and humidifies the air before delivering it through the floor void to a number of fan tile units (FTUs).

These are distributed throughout the space and provide the facility for local control of temperature and air flow by the occupant through a user adjusted thermostatically controlled damper and electric heater battery. They can be recessed into the floor void or floor mounted. The air is distributed from the CAM to the FTUs through separate supply and return air plena as opposed to ductwork.

Evaluation of environmental systems
The system is designed to maximise flexibility as FTUs can be relocated easily having no ductwork connections and integral thermostats, and the plena can be re-routed. However the success of such a strategy is dependent upon the speed of relocation of FTUs matching the churn rate and subsequent furniture location. In an open plan space with a large number of FTUs where churn is frequent it is possible for a user to either be surrounded by them or to be too far away from one for ease of control. In such a case users need to be encouraged to use their FTUs appropriately, eg if the occupants get too cold in summer due to excessive air movement they should either reduce the fan speed or increase the temperature of the air flow rather than turn the unit off completely.

If the floor void depth is minimised to take advantage of the plena approach the location of an additional CAM unit is important in case of upgrade as they need to be served by chilled water and linked to the main supply and extract system.

Within a closed cellular environment a *distributed* system is a good choice in terms of providing user control, although in an open plan environment close integration with the furniture system is needed. The ability to meet the diverse demand of the *club* could be questioned given the limited variation of conditioning possible through the user interface. The ease of maintenance offered by the system, ie the FTUs can be pulled out and replaced easily is considered essential to avoid disruption on the floor. CAM unit maintenance could be more disruptive. The ability to part operate the system is dependent upon the location of the FTUs relative to the CAM units.

15.4 Royal Bank of Scotland London, England

The organisation and its work patterns

The Waterhouse Square development is a modern extension to the Prudential Insurance complex in Holborn. The integration of the new extension with the older Prudential building has meant the office space occupied by Royal Bank of Scotland spreads across both building types. It has also meant that some of the utilities are supplied via Prudential and are often under their control rather than the Royal Bank of Scotland's. The 5 storey building, which retains the original Prudential facade, is built around two partially enclosed atria.

The office houses approximately 1000 staff in largely open plan accommodation. The functions of these staff fall into three main categories: the strategic management of the bank, international dealing, or support for the dealers. Small cellular offices are provided for some of the senior managers. Cellular meeting areas are also provided, ranging from small cellular rooms for 2 or 3 people around the atrium to boardroom style corporate meeting and entertaining facilities.

Lighting system

The artificial lighting is predominantly by Thorn Sensa overhead luminaires. The aim of the Sensa lighting control is to minimise the energy consumption associated with lighting whilst maintaining a comfortable light level. The Sensa device may include an occupant detector and a photocell to provide localised control of the fittings, allowing the lamps to be dimmed or switched depending on daylight penetration and occupant activity. The device can be integrated into some of the Thorn luminaire ranges or can be installed in to the in-fill between the luminaires.

An optional infra red hand held controller can also be used to provide individual control. Other benefits of the Sensa control include negating the need to install switch drops in the wiring circuits which not only saves on the installation costs of the system but also increases the flexibility to respond to churn within the office space.

Evaluation of the lighting system

The Waterhouse Square development uses a variety of switching methods depending on the location of the luminaires. Absence detection is used throughout the building, switching off all non-emergency lights when no occupants are detected. Luminaires adjacent to exterior or atria windows also include daylight switching. A dimming facility is built into the luminaires on the dealer floor, but user control has been withheld from the occupants.

Managers believe that providing the dealers with individual control would cause arguments in this densely populated area, and so dimming is carried out by the building managers on request. Whilst the absence detection and daylight switching have been accepted by the majority of the staff, the dimming control has proved to be unpopular amongst some of the dealers who have attempted to override some of the controls.

The control at Waterhouse Square has been configured so that the absence detection turns the lights off if an occupant has not been detected for approximately 45 minutes. This means that energy savings from this part of the control are largely through reduced lighting during out of hours periods, as few areas of an office of this size are unoccupied for this length of time during the working day.

16 Implications of the case studies:
learning from occupants' reactions

16.1 Introduction

The evaluations of the case studies by the project team were based on
- interviews with key technical and management personnel,
- contextual assessment based on the previous experience of the project team, and
- short term environmental monitoring.

In order to allow for a complete consideration of the appropriateness of the building and its services it was desirable to gather reactions to the buildings from the occupants. A systematic survey was not tenable within the restrictions of the project, since not all managers would agree to a survey and there was scope for involving only a small number of occupants in those buildings where managers did agree to a survey. Nevertheless, some impressions were gained through a combination of written questionnaires responses and the use of small focus group discussions.

The assessment of occupant reactions was designed to discover:
- Their awareness or perception of the importance of:
    i) environmental servicing (including lighting);
    ii) space planning and furniture selection in supporting an individual or organisational work pattern.
- If the assessments carried out by the project team during their brief visits to the building were in line with the views of the occupants. This is important if the guidance generated from the case studies is to be of general value.

16.2 Data collection and analysis

Between 20 and 30 occupant questionnaires were distributed in the buildings where management gave permission. The response rate varied greatly, with only 140 questionnaires returned in total from ten buildings. There can therefore be no claims that the information gathered from this exercise carries any degree of statistical validity. However it is important to realise that the intention of the analysis is to obtain indicative occupant reactions rather than precise measurements of (dis)satisfaction.

The data gathered here is of necessity fragile given that:
- causal relationships are difficult to isolate due to the interdependency of the variables under consideration,
- cross building comparisons accentuate the above as this interdependency will vary from building to building, and
- the number of responses, and the poor response rate, leave considerable potential for bias in the results (if, for example, those occupants who held extreme views were more likely to respond).

That said, when regarded with the appropriate level of scepticism, this form of information can provide a comparison with the other data collected in this study. Reassuringly, the results of these case study surveys proved to be supportive of previous work carried out by BRE and others.

The occupant questionnaire used appears in Appendix B, along with the questionnaires used in discussion with the technical and

management representatives. Results from the occupants have been analysed on the basis of 'normalised dissatisfaction'. Each question included in this analysis has an optimal, or zero dissatisfaction, answer. In some instances, questions have a mid point optimal, eg
Please rate the temperature on a typical summer's day:

Too hot	Fairly hot	Satisfactory	Fairly cold	Too cold

and in such questions, an individual's dissatisfaction can have a maximum absolute value of 2 (ie 2 boxes away from the optimal).

No differentiation is made between a response above or below the optimal value - frequently the direction of dissatisfaction is independent of the root cause of the problem. For example poor environmental servicing system performance can lead to one area of a building being too hot, whilst another is too cold. Equally, it can be argued that perceptions of hot and cold are adaptive and highly influenced by recent events. Thus it is more important to record the occurrence and level of dissatisfaction as opposed to its direction.

Other questions have an optimal at one end of the scale, taking the form:
Please rate the amount of distraction you experience from your work colleagues and their activities

No distraction	Rare distraction	Moderate distraction	A lot of distraction	Constant distraction

and clearly here the optimal response is 'no distraction'. Hence there is a maximum dissatisfaction rating of 4 (ie 'Constant distraction' is four boxes away from the optimal response).

By aggregating individual dissatisfaction levels, and then dividing by the maximum possible level of dissatisfaction that the respondees could have proffered, a normalised dissatisfaction response for the building is obtained. There are numerous statistical techniques that can be applied to the analysis of social questionnaire data. However the quantity of data obtained did not lend itself to a rigorous analytical exercise in view of the potential multiplicity of influencing factors.

The chosen normalised dissatisfaction method was a pragmatic approach developed for the study. The method has two key features:
- It is more representative of overall satisfaction than either the average (ie one response of 'too hot' and one response of 'too cold' have an average of 'satisfactory'), or the mode (all other responses are discarded).
- It eases cross comparison of the importance of individual variables within a building.

The final question of the survey asks the occupant to give a rating for the building as a whole.

When the case study buildings are ordered in terms of overall dissatisfaction as in Figure 121 the most noteworthy factors concerning the ordering are:
- There is no discernible relationship between defined work pattern and overall rating of the building.
- There is no discernible relationship between innovation of work pattern/space layout and the overall rating of the building.

Note that, as stated earlier, the vertical axis represents dissatisfaction so the lowest score represents the best building.

Recalling the four families of HVAC systems defined previously, it is interesting to observe the apparent influence that the system selection has upon perceived overall building performance (Figure 121).

On the admittedly limited evidence of the case study work there appeared to be a trend of 'occupant popularity' associated with types of HVAC systems - notably the preference for *mixed mode* systems followed by *distributed* and lastly *all air*. The one exception to this trend is the Gasunie building. As described earlier, the opulent architectural style of this building may means that it is atypical in that a 'compensatory effect' is occurring. Given the

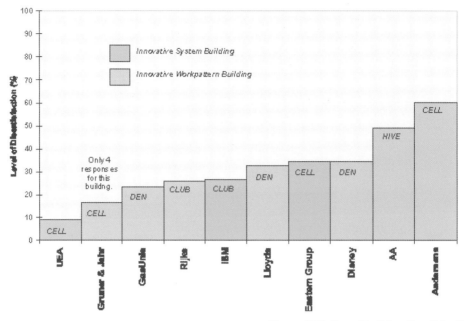

Figure 121 Overall building dissatisfaction levels

high cost of creating a building of this kind, it is not surprising that occupants respond positively overall.

Comparison between occupant opinions and project team assessments

Whilst the results from the occupant questionnaires appear to be consistent, it is essential that they are viewed against the assessments of the project team. Looking first at the overall performance of the building in relation to the specified HVAC system family the most popular six buildings evaluated have 'appropriate' affinities whilst the worst four are considered to be 'inappropriate' in relation to this study.

When the installation quality of a particular system is considered, that is how it is affected by the constraints which a particular building imposes upon the chosen system, there is also an encouraging level of consistency between occupant appraisals and project team assessments. Where differences occur they may be explained by the 'compensatory factors' involved in the specification of the space layout and interior design. For example the popularity of Gasunie (due to its opulent nature); the lower than expected rating for Anderson Consulting (due to the aged quality of the furniture and cramped surroundings which could not support the hotelling principle); or the higher than expected rating of Rijksgebouwendienst (attributable to the care taken with the furnishings, space planning of the *club* concept, and degree of user involvement in the development of the design concept, overcoming the relatively unsuitable HVAC servicing). However, clearly the ability to explain away any discrepancies between project team and user ratings needs to be regarded with caution. A closer inspection might identify discrepancies that explain those cases where there is consistency between the project team assessments and the occupant surveys.

Conclusions

The introduction of the concept of a linked 'environmental servicing and fit out quality' creates excellent consistency between the project team evaluations and the recorded occupant perceptions in the case studies. Such cohesion is consistent with the project team's view of the importance of the combination of environmental servicing, space planning and furniture selection in supporting the total quality of an individual or organisational workplace.

Overall Building Dissatisfaction Level

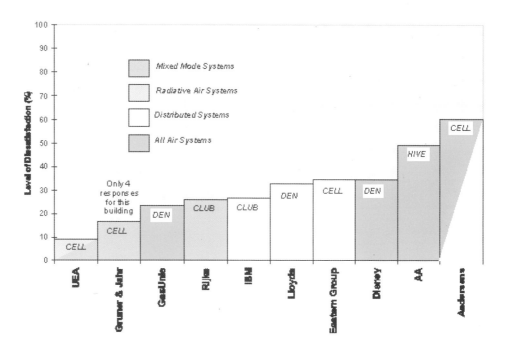

Figure 122 Overall building dissatisfaction level

Comparison of Objective Assessment of Appropriateness of Servicing Form and Occupant Dissatisfaction with Building

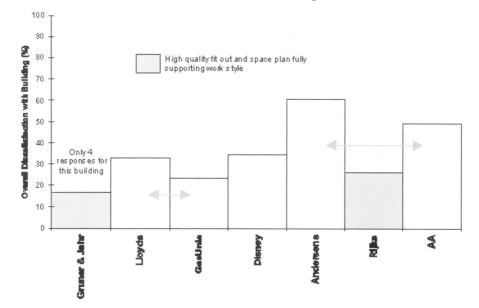

Figure 123 Comparison of project team assessment of 'appropriateness' of environmental servicing and occupant dissatisfaction with building

Part 5: Product directions and design implications

Drawing on the evaluations of the performance of environmental systems and building types in accommodating organisational demands, a series of directions for product development and design are highlighted. These address:

- building design and building management systems
- information technology
- HVAC systems and controls
- lighting
- space layout and furniture.

Part 1

Part 2

Part 3

Part 4

Part 5

Bibliography and appendices

17   Implications for the design of buildings and BMS

Summary of findings

From the exploration and evaluation described in previous chapters it is possible to hypothesise about the impact of new working patterns on the future of buildings. This chapter considers base building design, the specification of building management systems, and the implications for the building stock. Where relevant each area is discussed with reference to the requirements of the different procurement chain members.

It is anticipated that in developing the briefs for new or refurbished buildings individual clients or users will increasingly ask for:
- environmental systems that provide a higher degree of personalised individual and group control than is available at present, with the control interface being simpler and more accessible;
- much more consideration in the design of environmental systems to facilitate a transition from work patterns that are continuous and low in interaction to patterns of work which are certain to be quite the opposite;
- guidance to help avoid commissioning buildings which are too specifically designed for one particular work process;
- a sharper distinction between the level of environment provided for people spaces (which will tend to be for highly mobile, and changing groups), and for those areas which house support activities;
- the adaptive potential to shift the ratio between people and support zones over time, since the latter will tend to increase in many office organisations.

The onus on developers will be to:
- focus on producing simple straightforward *medium depth* and *atrium* office shells, avoiding both *shallow* and *deep plan* types except for specific purposes or client needs;
- ensure the simplest possible interfaces between environmental systems and building shells;

- allow enough space and volume to ensure adaptation to existing services, or to facilitate the provision of additional services in appropriate zones, eg a contingency or a zoned *mixed mode* approach;
- anticipate shorter leases and multi tenancies, and invent ways of providing effective shared common services for building occupants on a commercial basis, whilst permitting flexibility for each.

17.1 Implications for design briefs for buildings and building management systems (BMS)
Overall
- Space planning exercises demonstrate that the new working practices can effectively be placed into smaller units of office accommodation. The use of shared space will play an important role in this. The increased viability of smaller units will allow a much closer integration of offices into the urban fabric and open up their potential for use as other types of space.
- Mixed use buildings will become increasingly common as people seek to fully exploit their investment in property as a consequence of downsizing.
- *Deep plan central core* buildings and very *shallow* building types will be less usable except for a minority of *hive* organisations (*deep plan*) or the smaller *clubs* (*narrow plan*).
- *Medium depth* and *atrium* building configurations will best match the likely growth of *den* and *club* style organisations.
- The greater focus on the potential of *mixed mode* and *distributed* servicing systems to support *club* organisations is unlikely to reduce floor to floor ceiling heights because of longer term needs for the flexible locations of services. However, there may be an opportunity to design ceilings to take greater advantage of their exposed thermal mass. There are also opportunities afforded by locating *distributed* systems in the floor, ceilings, or on the walls.

- Building depth and configuration to permit natural ventilation within a *mixed mode* scenario will be a critical factor (and may only be possible in certain kinds of locations).

New office buildings

Office development has tended to produce large, homogeneous, isolated buildings. The implication of our argument is that exactly the opposite may be required for transactional *club* style organisations. That is smaller buildings, capable of accepting mixed uses, and linked together by a tissue of space, both internal and external, designed to encourage interaction. The model is not far to seek: it is the traditional city of streets, courts and alleyways.

At both the level of the workplace and of the office as a whole, the costs of increased capacity to accommodate a wider range of uses must be justified by the benefits of more effective programming of space use over time. However, this is only a fragment of the much more powerful economic arguments. Avoiding the penalties of space and layouts which prevent the new forms of work organisation, and achieving the benefits of new forms of layout which are in tune with the current revolution in organisational design, can be justified in such terms as the economic leverage provided by space use intensification.

Information technology

It is expected that the impact of innovations in information technology will make a wider range of buildings available for high quality use, given the declining physical and spatial impact of cables and the reduction in heat gain from IT equipment, as well as the growing opportunities offered by wireless communications. Nevertheless these opportunities will only be most successfully implemented in the most effective building types. The demands of central location will be somewhat marginalised by the mobile and nomadic nature of new ways of working supported by the space-less technologies of communication that are now becoming widespread.

17.2 The impact of re-thinking environmental services

Relation to base building design

The finding that *club* styles of organisation are best supported by *distributed* or *mixed mode* systems may have implications for base building design. The shift towards the *den* and ultimately the *club* with corresponding affinities to *distributed* and *mixed mode* systems suggests that architects and designers may wish to consider the latter as part of the future strategy for a building. This suggests building shells designed with a more integrated approach to overall building performance and which are less exclusive of the external environment.

Servicing technologies can be designed as selective additions rather than as blanket provision, although this would require the design to focus on more easily changed mechanical services that would complement and assist the natural ventilation. Central building systems will offer less of these opportunities than local and adaptable components. The use of mechanical options, at least in part, will allow the building depth to go beyond the traditional 15m limit previously associated with solely naturally ventilated buildings.

The flexibility of location of *distributed* HVAC systems, potentially in the floor, walls or ceiling spaces, provides opportunities to question floor to floor heights that have conventionally assumed both floor and ceiling voids for locations of cables and air or water distribution services. However, this is counterbalanced by the longer term needs of building occupants to sustain their capacity to alter and re-configure space and servicing which suggests that squeezing down floor to floor heights on the assumption that *distributed* systems can be fitted in more tightly is unwise. The dimensional impacts of these systems will vary, some requiring external wall locations others having central air distribution.

Building management systems

The implications for BMSs centre on their ability to carry out central supervision whilst allowing greater localisation of control at individual and group levels. However, in order for their powers to operate the building to suit the precise needs of an organisation to be fully exploited, the man-machine interface must be made as intuitive as possible to permit relatively untrained staff to make alterations on a more frequent basis.

The future BMS will be able to log how a building is being used, recognising patterns in occupancy profiles over a day, week, or year. It will predict the loads and react accordingly, for example to pre-cool an area of the building which is always occupied heavily at lunch time.

The BMS will be necessary to optimise plant control over the full range of occupancy and operating conditions experienced by the building eg a single person late night working, a move to flexi-time or seven day working. It will be able to control the interaction of various plant items such as chillers and fans to make the minimum energy decision, for example adjusting the degree of night cooling required if the building is to be occupied an hour earlier the next day.

Ceilings

Focusing on the most appropriate HVAC systems to support *den* and *club* patterns of work also provides opportunities for designers further to consider the role of ceilings. The potential exists for ceiling designs to:

- Exploit the benefits of thermal mass (and reduce the need for mechanical cooling) by increasing the exposed surface area with curves or other devices, also making it more aesthetically pleasing. This technique has already been used in buildings such as Powergen and the new Environmental Office at BRE.
- Provide shaped ceilings to direct their cooling effects to better support *radiative air* systems, although the impact on future flexibility must be borne in mind.

- Reduce the void size with certain HVAC systems, such as ATM zonal, or even to have no ceiling voids with systems such as the Hiross Flexible Space system which consists of under-floor fan coils.
- Re-define the needs for lighting (possibly uplighting) and structural ceiling finishes where suspended ceilings are no longer required.
- Make better provision for changes in layout in fast changing *den* or *club* type organisations, for example ease of demounting and integration of fixtures into ceiling tiles.
- Increased integration of the new *radiative air* technologies such as chilled beams and chilled ceilings.

Re-use of building stock

A straightforward adaptive approach for accommodating both environmental systems and information technology gives greater scope for the intelligent adaptive re-use of existing buildings. The mixed use of such existing structures is likely to become more possible. This recommendation is reinforced by our predictions that many organisations themselves will become smaller, more networked, more permeable, and more capable of using smaller buildings, and smaller floor plates to greater effect.

Within a larger building the floor space which is freed up by this may be let to tenants of a similar nature, or may be let to complementary organisations, eg a restaurant or leisure facility. It may also become space which is let to members of other organisations who are working in tandem, on a project which would benefit from team members being in the same location. An example of this might be a construction project where a team of engineers may relocate to the architect's premises for a short period.

18   Product directions for environmental systems

Summary of findings

The key strategic directions for environmental systems manufacturers to consider are to:

- Provide controls which are capable of responding to changing patterns of occupancy in a speedy, cost effective and energy efficient manner.
- Provide intelligent controls for individuals, teams and support spaces which allow maximum discretion for users and minimise operating costs, and which also greatly simplify the interface between the end user and the system.
- Develop strategies for effective *mixed mode* operations and focus on *distributed* systems because user demand for them is more likely to increase most quickly.
- Focus on how *radiative* and *all air* systems can be enhanced to be more suitable for the finer forms of control and responsiveness required by *den* and *club* organisations, and how they can be most effectively used within a *mixed mode* strategy.
- Enhance the effectiveness of maintenance routines through the use of advanced control and modelling techniques, and increase the ease of maintenance.

The following tables look at each of the HVAC system families in turn and consider how they might need to be improved on a generic level to fully meet the needs of each working pattern.

18.1 All air systems

VAV + radiator perimeter heating	VAV + terminal re-heat	Fan assisted VAV	Low temp fan assisted VAV	Dual duct air conditioning (constant volume)

Den	**Club**
Occupancy detection to minimise wastage in unoccupied spaces Variable fresh air rates (improved air quality control)	Increased ability to cope with zonal diversity Improved zoning and individual control On line maintenance with minimal down time Occupancy detection to minimise wastage in unoccupied spaces Variable fresh air rates (improved air quality control) Improved mixing and avoidance of short circuiting
Hive	**Cell**
Improved mixing and avoidance of short circuiting	Improved zoning and individual control On line maintenance with minimal down time

Figure 124 Work pattern demands on *all air* HVAC systems

Overview on product development directions

● An examination of the possibilities of low temperature VAV systems and their ability to accommodate the diversity associated with a *club* environment, whilst reducing the normal space implications of air based systems. However, low temperature systems may accentuate the problem of downdraughts from a lack of throw of the diffuser at low air speeds.

● An examination of the realised long term performance of air quality control methods (eg CO_2 or occupancy based) for *all air* systems serving the *den, cell* and *club* environments.

● A look at automated preventative maintenance to minimise the downtime associated with *all air* systems.

● The requirements of the *cell* and *club* may be achievable through the application of desk based personal ventilation systems, although their performance remains to be explored in any detail. They currently appear to have a somewhat expensive image, and have not really been adopted yet in the UK as a main servicing solution.

18.2 Radiative air systems

Mechanical displacement vent. + perimeter heating	Mechanical displacement vent. + static heating and cooling	Ventilating chill/heat beams	Hollow core ventilation system

Den	**Club**
Occupancy detection to minimise wastage in unoccupied spaces Avoidance of office rain due to variable occupancy density	Improved knowledge on achieved performance Significantly greater individual control Greater ability to maintain internal conditions thereby allowing improved individual control Faster response Occupancy detection to minimise wastage in unoccupied spaces Avoidance of office rain due to variable occupancy density
Hive	**Cell**
Improved knowledge on achieved performance - in principle these represent an ideal system	Significantly greater individual control needed Greater ability to maintain internal conditions thereby allowing improved individual control Faster response

Figure 125 Work pattern demands on *radiative air* HVAC systems

Overview on product development directions:

- A review of the realised performance of *radiative air* systems (which are already considered as highly innovative by the UK building services industry) through EC case studies. There are a limited number of such systems in this country, although those that exist are receiving a large amount of press attention. UK designers are in need of independent definitive design information.
- An evaluation of the opportunities for improved individual control of *radiative air* systems, with infra-red controllers being one possibility.
- An examination of the maintenance implications of *radiative air* systems, eg cleaning.

18.3 Distributed systems

Four-pipe fan coil units + central ventilation	ATM Zonal AC	Terminal heat with central vent.	Induction units	VRF cooling system	Hiross (or similar) under floor system

Den	**Club**
Tighter control ability (remote sensing, smaller sawtooth etc)	Tighter control ability (remote sensing, smaller sawtooth etc)
Ability to match diverse loads and maintain a high COP	Ability to match diverse loads and maintain a high COP
Improved user interface control	Improved user interface control
Acoustic and mechanical isolation needed	Acoustic and mechanical isolation needed
Occupancy detection to minimise wastage in unoccupied spaces	Occupancy detection to minimise wastage in unoccupied spaces
Reduction of design and installation cost	Reduction of design and installation cost
Hive	**Cell**
Generally inappropriate assuming large open plan spaces	Only suitable for highly cellularised *cell* activities or in shallow depth plan

Figure 126 Work pattern demands on *distributed* HVAC systems

Overview on product development directions

● The poor ranking of certain *distributed* systems (which, in the modelling exercise, appeared well suited to the *den*, *club* and possibly *cell* environments) justifies examination of the perceived practical barriers to their successful application.

● An examination of the use of perimeter *radiative* cooling (ie the summertime equivalent of a radiator heating system) for *cell* or *den* activity in *narrow plan* buildings.

18.4 System family: tempered air (leading to mixed mode)

Window vent + radiator perimeter heating	Facade vent. and perimeter heating	Mechanical extract vent, window supply and radiator heating	Mechanical supply and extract + radiator heating

Den	**Club**
Suitable for *den*/cellular areas but need to consider impact of extended occupancy hours on viability Likely to need provision for a supplementary cooling system Controllable means of providing air quality control through opening windows	*Mixed mode* approach is particularly suitable for diverse *club* requirements Need to supplement with localised cooling if space use intensification occurs Avoidance of "preferred" window seats Limitations on night cooling etc. due to extended occupancy periods Suitable for *den/cell* areas but need to consider impact of extended occupancy hours on viability Controllable means of providing air quality control through opening windows
Hive	**Cell**
Generally inappropriate assuming large open plan spaces but could be utilised for communal/rest areas	Need to supplement with localised cooling if space use intensification Avoidance of "preferred" window seats Limitations on night cooling etc. due to extended occupancy periods

Figure 127 Work pattern demands on tempered air HVAC systems

Overview on product development directions

- The popularity of natural ventilation with occupants implies that consideration of *mixed mode* systems whenever possible is advisable, particularly in the *club* environment. However strategic guidance is needed on the design of such systems to ensure that they return in practice the degree of flexibility, economic benefit, and user satisfaction that in theory they should offer.
- A consideration of the interaction between active and passive systems (particularly *radiative air* systems where there is a fear of condensation risk, and *all air* or *distributed* systems to ensure appropriate interlocks with window operation).
- An examination of ways of overcoming the apparent 'preferential treatment' for near window occupants.
- An examination of the performance of various forms of automatic window control gear, which in the past have not been totally reliable.

18.5 Product direction conclusions

The driving forces for change arise from four major sets of interests:

- **The users**: needing a greater degree of individual or group control, and systems that are simple to operate.

- **The client organisation**: needing systems that necessitate the least disruption to the business process due to maintenance, whether this is because the specified system actually requires less maintenance, the maintenance can be carried out more easily, or because it can be carried out externally to the occupied space.

- **The owner**: needing the ability to upgrade, re-arrange or refurbish the office space to meet the requirements of shorter leases, changing tenant and occupier requirements, and responding to the needs of multi-tenanted buildings.

- **The designer**: needing to ensure that the design can operate effectively over the full range of the building operating conditions anticipated now, or in the future.

The directions for product development can be seen as focusing on the following key areas:
- Controls
- Maintenance
- Modularity and flexibility
- Commissioning.

Controls

In terms of developments in available controls, the main requirements generated by the new working patterns are seen as being:

- The ability to respond to changing patterns of occupancy in a cost effective and economic manner without adversely affecting the quality of the environment of the staff who remain more permanently in the space, in particular in open plan offices.

- The possibility of providing a greater degree of control, on an individual or team level, which will not adversely affect the quality of environment for adjacent individuals or staff.

- The ability to understand the operation of the controls provided so that full advantage can be taken of the opportunities offered by a control system to match the change in an organisation's operation.

- Intelligent controls that will result in the optimum use of energy and minimum operating cost, but which greatly simplify the interface with the user.

- Improved predictive control algorithms that will be able to cope with the uncertain nature of modern working patterns.

Examples of how this is being, or might be, applied include:

- Intelligent fan control that will optimise the choice of air flow rate and supply temperature to achieve the minimum energy use, coupled with the availability of good quality inexpensive variable speed fans. Methods of doing this can be investigated using operational research techniques. It is important that this is achievable using actual fan and chiller efficiencies, rather than average performance curves, to allow control to be site specific.

- The use of CO_2 sensing or occupancy control as a way of linking air flow rates to the actual requirements for fresh air within a space. Carbon dioxide is supposedly a useful indicator of general levels of indoor air pollution and ventilation effectiveness, as it is a gas which can be monitored to an appropriate level of accuracy and accounts, in some measure, for the actual occupancy within a space. It may also be possible to control directly to people numbers if entry into a room or space could be satisfactorily registered. An example of its application would be in a *den* type environment where a team meeting may lead to greater requirements for fresh air within an area for that time only. Both these methods would need to be linked to a fast response HVAC system.

- Methods for enhancing user control could involve the development of simpler interfaces, eg for a BMS system to allow a facilities manager to interact fully with the system and rearrange lighting schedules for out of hours working. Interfaces may also be developed to indicate to a user the consequences of his or her actions. For example with a system dependent upon the use of exposed thermal mass if the user chooses to increase the air flow rate into the space the coolth stored within the slab will be expended before the end of the working day, and may necessitate using a supplementary cooling system. The system could forewarn the facilities manager of this.

- The development of personal desk ventilators is a move towards integrating environmental systems and their controls with the furniture, thereby making controls more accessible, and providing the ultimate in individual control. However work still needs to be carried out on the interaction between the localised and central plant, and calculating the realised energy savings.

- Echelon chip control can be fitted to a variety of plant items to provide them with localised enhanced intelligence. An echelon chip is designed to be a distributed low power consumption microprocessor, which is cheap enough to potentially be installed on a room by room or item by item basis. They are currently fitted in certain light fittings and fire alarm systems. However they could, for example, also be fitted to chilled ceiling valves and associated local humidistats, or window actuators and local temperature sensors to provide local intelligent control of a *radiative air* based *mixed mode* system. This would avoid unnecessary reference back to the BMS and would allow less cabling and hence greater ease of installation.

Maintenance

Developments in this area to meet the needs of the new ways of working are based on:
- The ability to maintain equipment more easily, for example easy clean coils and ductwork, or modular equipment which allows replacement units to be slotted in while faulty equipment is taken away and repaired off site. This may be of particular importance in an enclosed version of a working pattern where there is consequently no opportunity for the other units to compensate.

- The ability to predict maintenance requirements and react to them prior to plant failure.

- The ability for a controller of a plant item to react to a degradation in performance of that item by compensating for it effectively, for example changing valve characteristics to account for wear and tear.

Examples of how these principles might be delivered include:
- The use of anti-microbial coatings for filters and ductwork which has been investigated within the military field, and is to be examined for use within the building services industry.

- Systems such as ATM zonal where the only items which would require access from within the occupied space are flexible ducting and ceiling diffusers. The items of mechanical plant are located in distributed plant rooms, although this has space implications.

- Condition based maintenance is a strategy most suited for plant items which are critical to the operation of a particular system, and for which the costs in terms of lost business due to failure or the cost of replacement is great. It is based upon monitoring various parameters which are considered indicative of the plant item performance, eg vibration levels, power consumption, or a lubricant analysis, where any deviation in the pre-set value or performance characteristics is an indicator that attention is needed. It will also be possible to produce the most cost effective maintenance schedule, eg one which takes account of the cost of bringing in an engineer and optimises repair times accordingly. Techniques such as this can be applied to *club* type environments where the impact of plant failure may be most damaging, or in certain *hive* type environments which rely heavily upon centralised IT equipment such as data processing or financial companies where a failure of the computing system due to overheating could be catastrophic.

- The detection of faults in building services is necessary in order to optimise energy consumption, maintain occupant comfort and minimise operating costs. Problems such as valve leakage and sensor drift may not be easily recognisable, and can lead to long term energy wastage. Fault detection models are being developed which allow the correct plant operation to be compared with actual operation and possible causes for any differences to be identified and reported. This development is beneficial across all the working patterns.

- The above developments involve the use of various artificial intelligence devices such as neural networks, a novel form of computer algorithm which is able to draw conclusions from incomplete sets of data through mimicking certain processes of the human brain. These algorithms can also be used to compensate for any faults which are detected due to wear and tear of plant, and poor commissioning. The technology (being software based) should ultimately be inexpensive and simple to install. The intelligence of the neural network allows it to determine whether it can improve on the performance of the basic controller, and it will only initiate a control modification if it can do so. Hence this is a low risk advance which offers the potential to enhance occupant comfort and to produce energy savings.

- If plant is to become more modular with a tendency for items to be become smaller it will become more appropriate for equipment to become 'plug in and pull out', for example the fan tile units of the Hiross system, or the ATM boxes. This approach will benefit the *club* type organisation with its more rapidly changing needs.

Commissioning

Key areas for improvement in commissioning techniques include:

- Self balancing air and water systems which minimise the need for recommissioning effort following a system upgrade or change to the layout, for example the development of a high quality constant volume device.

- Improved grille and diffuser design to ensure that the desired air flow paths occur with minimum pressure drops and noise generation regardless of the loading on the system.

- Techniques for balancing void based systems.

19 Implications for lighting

Summary of findings

Many of the design philosophy issues which can be applied to lighting systems to match the need of the new working patterns parallel developments needed for HVAC systems. Lighting designers and manufacturers should, for example, consider:

● The demands raised by different work patterns for lighting products, such as:
  - lighting to support 24 hour shift and night time working (*hive*);
  - a much greater opportunity for intelligent individual and team control of lighting features through the BMS or universal personalisable controllers (*cell, den,* and *club*);
  - more multi-task adjustable task lighting to suit shared settings (*club*);
  - better fine tuning of occupancy sensing where occupancy patterns may be erratic, extended and unpredictable (*cell, den,* and *club*).

● The lighting needs raised by new forms of communication such as:
  - video communications whether the technology is linked to a desktop PC, or sited in a separate room;
  - developments in IT screen technologies such as new screen coatings or horizontal screens.

● Better integration of the lighting and HVAC design strategies with each other, for example to avoid the lights acting as a detrimental source of heat.

● Integration of the lighting with the base building, for example, designing for an exposed mass ceiling whereas conventional office lighting systems typically assume suspended false ceilings.

19.1 Work pattern demands for lighting

The work patterns described in this study are associated not only with typical kinds of space layout, but also with patterns of owned, shared, and temporary space use. The work pattern models suggest the potential for sharing of space over time across all of the four types, but with some key differences. In the *hive* work pattern, the sharing of space over time is typically associated with shift work (diachronic); in the *cell, den,* and *club* other simultaneous patterns of sharing or space use intensification are possible (synchronic).

The way in which space is shared and the correlation of the work pattern with different kinds of layout present a range of product implications and design directions for lighting. William Bordass (1996) has explored some of these issues in other work for BRE. His conclusions have been examined below in the context of the *hive, cell, den* and *club* model.

Space management	Work pattern	Space layout	Pattern of sharing
Owned	CELL	open plan or enclosed	NA
	HIVE	open plan	NA
Temporarily owned	HIVE	open plan	shift work
	CELL	open plan or enclosed	time share
	DEN	open plan or group room	time share
	CLUB	open and enclosed	
Shared	DEN	open plan or group room	time share
			shared space

Figure 128 Space management, work patterns, space layout and pattern of sharing

Space ownership	Characteristics	Examples	Typical issues and problems	Suitable approaches
Owned	Occupants regard the space as their own, and want to make their own decisions about the status of the lights. A close relationship between user, space and control makes this possible.	Small offices for 1 and 2 persons.	Occupants need to switch lights both on and off, and greatly object to 'Big Brother' controls. Any automatic adjustments should be imperceptible to them (eg. absence-sensing once the room is vacated, or gradual dimming).	Avoid automatic switch-on. Light switches by the door can be used effectively. Consider absence-seeking and photoelectric dimming to avoid waste. Always provide local over-ride.
Shared	Occupants regard their part of the space as their own but cannot be in full control of environmental systems which have to suit others as well. Ideally there should be some local control, or failing that task lighting available on request.	Open-plan offices and group rooms.	Systems default to convenient but inefficient states. This is typically with all the lights on. The status then only changes if the situation becomes intolerable, or at the end of the day.	Separate control (and identification) of lighting for circulation, decoration and safety avoids the first arrival switching on everything. Ideally have local switching and adjustment at individual workstations. Consider 'last-out, lights out' facility.
Temporarily owned	Occupants are usually present for a few hours at a time. They can be in individual or consensus control while they are there, but they may not be very familiar with the controls. Lights are left on when the rooms are vacated: nobody feels responsible.	Meeting rooms, quiet rooms, study carrels, lab writing up areas, project areas.	Controls are not easy enough to find or understand. Presence detection is misused in meeting rooms by omitting local over-ride for slide presentations etc. Nuisance triggering of presence-detectors, hence manual 'on' is often preferable.	Highly-visible easy-to-understand local controls in obvious places. Absence sensing is desirable, preferably with last-out, lights-out facility at the exit. Teaching and presentation rooms may require dimming and control from the lectern.

Figure 129 Implications of space ownership and management for lighting (source: William Bordass)

Trends

Lighting is frequently the largest single item of energy expenditure in UK offices, accounting for about 35% of energy costs. Hence the importance, regardless of the working pattern in place, of making improvements in this area, as well as considering the contribution lighting makes to the provision of a safe, comfortable and productive work environment. Designers cannot ignore:
- the balance between local and central, or manual and automatic, controls as work place layouts develop,
- the role of task lighting,
- the role of occupancy sensing,
- the impact of partitioning,
- the impact of new technology.

Lighting control systems and task lighting

Recent case study work by BRE has shown the performance of lighting control systems to generally fall short of expectations. It has been suggested that this is due to the changing nature of offices, in particular deep plan spaces with extensive VDU use, and a failure to tailor the control system to match the needs of both staff and management. Extended building operating hours will change the economics of applying lighting control measures due to the attendant energy implications.

Greater consideration will need to be paid to unowned areas such as corridors and meeting spaces, where no one has the responsibility for the control of the lights. If the office of the future contains less personal space those areas, which are not the personal responsibility of someone, will increase. Corridor lighting tends to be over-bright for its function and people entering the office space from the corridor may feel it to be too dim and switch on additional lights.

New ways of working suggest greater reliance on local occupant control as far as possible, given the unpredictability and diversity of occupancy patterns. Occupants in the *club* type of office (or any other working pattern which has introduced hot desking) may be unfamiliar with the space, layout and control systems, hence the need for devices which can be readily understood and easily used. The requirement for greater individual occupant control will be further supported by the increasing diversity of tasks undertaken by groups and individuals demanding more

variable lighting conditions. This suggests a greater focus on task lighting which would be designed for multi-tasking in the same space by different people with individual preferences.

The development of intelligent fittings (eg containing echelon chips) that can be programmed on an individual basis has opened up unlimited possibilities for flexibility. Straightforward time based systems are becoming more difficult to use with the increase in flexitime operation. If buildings are to be occupied by more than one company the lighting system must be easily programmable to account for their differing needs. The lighting management systems software should be user friendly to allow the maximum benefit to be gained from the system.

The growth of office shift-working (24 hour telesales or information services for example)demands more focus on lighting products for night-time and extended periods of use. There is a need to encourage people to close blinds at night both for thermal reasons and to improve the general internal light level whilst minimising external light pollution. The design of lighting systems should be linked to internal blind operation or other forms of window covering appropriate for night time work. To provide visual interest through contact with the outside world it may be appropriate to compromise through lowering alternate blinds or closing blinds at the top of each window only.

Experiences from 24 hour working such as security operations leads to a consideration of ways of maintaining arousal, for example through changing light levels. Given the lack of day lighting the colour rendering of artificial lighting becomes more significant. A further consequence of extended hours working is the reduced time for maintenance to be carried out within the occupied space.

Different emphasis on the building versus the task lighting provision may be associated with individual work patterns. Greater emphasis on task lighting is associated with higher levels of variability of tasks and with greater expectations for individual control. Both of these characteristics are more likely in the *cell* and *club* environments rather than the *den* and the *hive*. On the other hand, in both *hive* and *den* the provision of task

	Building	Task
Overall needs	Surface brightness and ambience	Micro environment for the user
Lighting provision	Uplight	Uplight
	Wall light	Local task light,
	Suspended up/down	or suspended up/down
	dimmable	dimmable

Figure 130 Variable building and task lighting demands

lighting is one of the easiest ways of providing higher levels of individual control in environments that are otherwise typically more centralised or consensus based in their servicing provision.

The use of smaller work corrals for individual working can lead to more reliance on task lighting to avoid the shadowing effects caused by partitioning combined with general lighting. If staff are spending time in these small working areas they will need to have a point in the distance to focus on to allow their eyes to relax.

The role of occupancy sensing
Occupancy sensing - both presence and absence detection - has been introduced into offices in recent years. Presence detectors can cause problems in open plan areas or in meeting rooms, although they are more suited to small enclosed spaces. Ultrasonic and passive infra-red devices can pick up movement and thermal currents from air conditioning vents so their positioning must be thought out. They must be set to take into account the presence of even one person in an open area/meeting room, especially if meeting rooms will double up as spare office space in organisations where space sharing has been introduced to a high degree.

Rather than presence detection with auto switch-off it may be better to consider manual switch-on linked to absence detection. This will minimise the embarrassment of lights switching off in meetings, but could pose problems for areas with ad hoc partitioning. Sensors must be positioned so that someone passing the open door of an office or walking past a team work space does not trigger the lighting.

The impact of partitioning
Partitioning affects daylight penetration into the space and the lighting system must allow for this and any future changes to the office layout. Furniture which appears above the nominal working plane of about 0.75m can also affect lighting distribution. Sensor positions should be selected with care to take into account the effect of partitioning on the adequate provision of appropriate lighting levels, layout flexibility, and control by occupancy sensing.

The impact of new technology
Appropriate lighting for video conferencing via the personal computer at the individual work setting needs to be considered. This will require the capacity to be switched on manually or automatically whenever this service is accessed on the computer (the lighting will be the local equivalent of studio lighting). Lighting should be at the correct angle for the screen image and present good colour rendering. This requirement will be needed both for individual and for group ancillary use.

Changes in screen format will support a shift to greater tolerance of screens for reflection. Flat screen and A4 tablets will reduce the problem of glare and reflection, permitting greater flexibility in the location and layout of work settings adjacent to window areas.

Lighting product directions

Controls for club style work patterns
● Develop a standard hand held controller for lighting that could be used everywhere and which would be familiar to all office users, similar to a TV remote controller.

● Develop a PC based control system which the user can log into. The system would know what it is possible to do, and what the individual user likes to do. It would tell the user what lighting or other environmental systems are available and how to control them. Another version of this facility could be where the room or space is programmed to recognise the individual user and responds by activating the environment to suit the individual's preferences. Product development is already happening in this area.

● Develop lighting management system software to sum the decisions of groups working together to optimise the environmental conditions that would suit the group (appropriate in the *den* offices).

● Take advantage of Echelon chip technology (or similar) to expand the range of intelligent fittings and allow more highly tailored programming.

● Consider techniques to provide suitable lighting for both VDU and non-VDU users within the same open plan space.

● Consider the integration of lighting and furniture systems, for example the positioning of task lighting.

Base lighting systems
● A base lighting system infrastructure that can be upgraded and downgraded to suit the requirements of changing work patterns (from *hive*, to *den*, to *cell*, to *club*).

● Develop base lighting systems in relation to the different design strategies associated with the families of HVAC system outlined in this study (*all air, radiative air, distributed, mixed mode*). Investigate whether there is potentially one base lighting system that can be used with all such families of systems and which can allow change between different patterns of use over time.

● Can the base lighting strategy be linked to a base wiring system?

● The proposed base systems should allow for sensors to be robust and capable of easy relocation to suit the needs of changing layouts and work pattern demands (allow for changes to zoning). Re-positioning of elements without damage to ceilings or other fit out elements will be required.

Lighting design linked to base building design
● The affinity between *mixed mode* and *distributed* HVAC systems with the *club* and *den* work patterns may correlate with lighting design issues. For example the potential to relocate servicing elements away from a ceiling zone may mean more attention will need to be paid to lighting designs for structural ceiling elements rather than for suspended ceilings.

● There may be links between lighting design approach chosen and the emergence of new forms of glazing such as electro and photochromic.

External daylight control
● External modulation of daylight and sunshine (light shelves, louvres, blinds, or other devices) may be linked to *mixed mode* approaches as extensive efforts have been made to reduce the dependence upon active means of servicing.

● The relationship of external lighting control at the building perimeter may conflict with other forms of local or group control associated with patterns of use in the interior of the building. The affinities between building depth and configuration and work patterns explored in this study will also therefore have an impact on the expectations for lighting design and control.

20 Implications for space layout and furniture

Summary of findings

Furniture manufacturers should:

- Focus on specifying furniture products that support interactive, collaborative, intermittent work processes alongside, and in conjunction with, spaces for individual concentrated work (both with and without the use of IT).
- Develop furniture systems which can enhance individual and team control of the working environment.
- Expand the conventional boundaries of office furniture and interiors components to enhance partitions, ceilings, and access floors in order to provide a better and more flexible interface between organisations, buildings and environmental systems.
- Develop new boundaries for products that would serve to support organisations seeking to make the transition from the *hive* to *den*, the *cell* to *den*, and the *den* to *club* styles of office. These products may be tools, accessories, and management systems, as much as conventional furniture. They will serve to upgrade and transform both the spatial quality of the environment and the ways in which it is used.

20.1 Directions for change

What is striking is how very different the new ways of working are to the old. This is best explained in an analysis of what the conventional office looks like and what it means.

Conventional offices:

- only work on the basis of one person per workstation, and then only from nine to five;
- are excellent at expressing boundaries;
- are even better at reinforcing hierarchy;
- suit big groups rather than small;
- do not support teamwork;
- offer limited settings;
- are ideal for clerical tasks;
- accept IT only with the greatest difficulty.

The office for new ways of working

The old office design conventions seem extraordinarily hard to change. Each conventional element in the vocabulary of office design:

- workstations
- screens
- storage
- partitions
- building services

is presently configured to prevent innovation. Each element insists on its own logic – which tends to be that of the supplier rather than the user. How can this logic be broken? The key elements will be:

- Fewer individual workstations; much more shared accommodation. The workstation will become more focused on permitting one-one interaction and will be in close proximity to areas for group activity. Focused individual concentrated work will occur away from the personal workstation in shared spaces specialised for this purpose and used temporarily.

- Ways in which the conventional workstation can be transformed and re-configured to support new patterns of work that are more interactive, more intermittent, and less sedentary. The workstation becoming more like a work bench to which are attached various additional pieces that serve to change its functionality as the need arises.

- Far wider range of settings ancillary to the individual space or which indeed replace the individual space, these will include:
  - quiet rooms for concentrated work and thought;
  - more specialised spaces and facilities for presentation and display, using both paper and electronic means and which can be integrated into the normal team work space (not segregated into separate formal presentation suites);
  - new forms of storage that support easy and efficient access for group tools and files and which do not depend on individually 'owned' positions;

- new ways of using incidental, intermediary, circulation spaces to make them vital contributors to nomadic interactive work styles, integrating display functions and communication tools, (phone, fax, computers). Such spaces will provide 'quick stop' facilities for spontaneous meetings and quick work discussions. They will enable people to immediately 'pick up' information or access data and news and see what is going on. They can also be used for breaks, informal relaxing and hanging out with colleagues. These spaces will become more important as the work process is more nomadic and the office as a whole becomes a place of serendipitous exchange or transaction of ideas, views, and knowledge.

● Greater proportion of support spaces – in fact, by the whole office becoming a mixture of transactional and support spaces.

● Fewer screens, more partitions that divide and define zones of activity, less for individual ownership, more for a wide range of shared individual and group tasks.

● Greater diversity in mood, style and image.

The *club* office may incorporate elements of:
  - the domestic environment: the informal interaction of the kitchen table, the relaxed atmosphere of the family *den*;
  - the workshop or laboratory, where new technologies are used experimentally, where knowledge is advanced through testing and risk taking;
  - the airport lounge, where the traveller can quickly re-charge, access tools and information, and maintain contact with the world within a totally shared and semi-public space;
  - the stage or film set and the art gallery installation, where a powerful even if transient image can be created to stimulate a specific culture or reinforce a strong identity;
  - the hotel, where the guest room can be highly serviced and tailored to the temporary needs of the individual;
  - the retreat, where the individual goes alone to contemplate.

● new kinds of products outside of the normal purview of 'furniture' that will enhance and transform the environment:
  - support for the use of IT in collaborative and team settings;
  - portable storage devices;
  - presentation tools and equipment for interactive work;
  - management training and services to support shared space use and space use intensification;
  - ways of enhancing the acoustic privacy of spaces when used for interaction or conference calls with speaker phones.

We can translate these changes in demand into the more particular characteristics of the work patterns identified in this study.

Den	Club
The style of the office reinforces the group; the mode is group space; the scale medium to small; the geography tending to dispersal; the logic social; the timetable extended.	The style of the office is collegial; the mode *club* like; ie offering choice of a wide variety of settings for different purposes; the scale is medium and stable; the geography central; the logic transactional; the timetable increasingly complex depending on what has to be done as well as on individual arrangements.
Expect: differentiated complex workstations; strongly marked boundaries within open plan or group rooms; medium filing; elaborated ways of generating group interactions – meeting tables, meeting rooms; more emphasis on direct face to face contact within – electronic contact beyond group boundaries.	**Expect:** a wide range of settings both open and enclosed; few individual workstations; much sharing; elaborate and constantly changing IT; a widening range of meeting, teaching, interaction spaces; some social facilities.
Next steps: a swift progression towards the *club* as IT and artificial intelligence rapidly enhances group competence. Increasing instability of boundaries.	**Next steps:** much greater emphasis on searching for better ways of relating to consultants, clients, non core staff, eg elaborate training areas; use of other urban facilities – restaurants, cafes. Virtual officing and telepresence.
Hive	**Cell**
The style of the office is corporate; the mode is open plan; the scale tends to be large; the geography concentrated in one place; the logic engineering; the timetable conventional but tending to shift work.	The style of the office is individualistic but within a powerful corporate frame; the mode is highly cellular; the scale is medium and declining; the geography tending to dispersed; the logic monastic; the timetable increasingly ragged, dependent on individual arrangements.
Expect: ganged, minimalist workstations; minimal partitions; maximal filing; structured cabling; elaborate break areas and social facilities to boost morale; devices to engender competitive team spirit.	**Expect:** highly cellular accommodation allowing individual discretion within; elaborated IT; a range of meeting spaces and some social facilities.
Next steps: increasing power of automation will lead to reduction in paper filing; homeworking; and eventual elimination – unless the *hive* is transformed into *den*.	**Next steps:** hotelling tending towards home working or towards the *club*.

Figure 131 Trends in furniture and layout associated with work patterns

Den	Club
Expect: space standards: space allocation determined by the group; layout: complex and continuous, combining individual workstations with meeting tables; boundaries: fluid, tendency towards continuity of worktop; servicing: worktops independent of each other and of service distribution – service walls; ergonomics: up to the individual; style: familial and interactive. **Next steps:** Increasing need to accommodate a wider range of types of work, equipment and work practices; increasing pressure on space. Inherently expensive.	**Expect:** space standards: irrelevant; layout: diverse, complex and manipulable; boundaries: used to differentiate between different settings; servicing: independent of furniture layout; ergonomics: hardly critical; style: varied and changeable. **Next steps:** Increasingly virtual; potential to be shared by more than one organisation; use of alternative central city and other locations; differentiation of *club* type locations by style, image and status; relationship to tele-working reinforced.
Hive	**Cell**
Expect: space standards: imposed – once elaborate, now simpler; layout: ganged workstations in pairs, four packs, six packs, etc; boundaries: often highly marked between workstations; servicing: integrated; ergonomics: critical; style: corporate. **Next steps:** Increasing reduction of amount of space as well as choice at the level of the footprint countered by increasing ergonomic choice at the level of detailed design. High unit costs and space squandering leading to eventual phasing out. Inherently obsolete.	**Expect:** space standards: complete uniformity; layout: remorselessly rigid exterior, high discretion interior; boundaries: sharply marked, often screened or enclosed; servicing: integrated; ergonomics: the ergonomics of the airplane seat; style: corporate and impersonal exterior, individual interior. **Next steps:** Uniformity likely to break down under the pressure of demand for more complex pattern of work.

Figure 132 Trends in furniture and layout associated with work patterns

21 The impact of software

21.1 Introduction

This chapter has been provided by Robert Worden, formerly of Logica. In it he analyses how developments in IT, particularly in software, will change the way people work and thus affect their working environment. Rather than just reach a few headline conclusions, he has surveyed and evaluated ongoing business and technical developments and pointed to likely outcomes in several areas; readers are invited to assess and prioritise these for themselves. This chapter was originally drafted in 1996 and is reproduced here with only slight updating. It is both interesting and gratifying to note the validity of many of the author's original predictions.

While developments in raw technology are sometimes easy to predict, the changes in the application of technology are much harder to foresee, since they depend on many commercial, business and social factors—and in particular, often follow from a 'snowball effect' in which some specific application catches the public imagination and spawns many imitators. Predicting when a snowball will start to roll is almost impossible. Partly for this reason, it is best to start not from technology developments, but from changes in the business environment.

This chapter is therefore organised in the following sections:
Business drivers: key features and changes in the current business environment which provide a market pull for certain applications of IT, more than for others.

How IT will change the way people work: Some generic application areas which are fast becoming technically feasible (or are already so) and which mesh with the changes in the business environment, to alter work patterns.

Technology enablers: Key developments in hardware and (mainly) in software which will underpin these applications.

Blocking factors: Factors which are expected to inhibit progress towards the applications and the changes.

Each section consists of a list of key changes or developments, with a brief description of each. From this collection of ideas it is possible to sketch a typical work pattern for a knowledge worker in a leading-edge company in the early part of the next Milennium.

21.2 Business drivers

Some key changes are evident in the business climate over recent years, for example:

Customer orientation
In the immediate post-war years, the key objectives of large businesses were concerned with scale, cost and control. In recent years there has been a marked change of emphasis towards quality and customer satisfaction (initiated largely by Japanese successes in consumer goods, themselves inspired by the Deming/Duran quality messages). Today, in order to succeed, nearly all businesses recognise their need to maximise quality, to be more responsive to individual customers, and increasingly also to their own staff. This amounts to a massive change in business priorities.

Broadcast to narrowcast
It seems likely that changes in computer and communications technology (particularly cable into the home, the Internet and its successors) will alter the balance of commercial advantage away from large organisations which can broadcast their message to many (via newspaper and television advertising) in favour of much smaller, specialist providers of goods and services, which customers can pro-actively search for and find out about over world-wide networks. Customers are increasingly empowered to select what they want to see, hear or read, rather than accept it from the large corporations who can buy their attention.

Quality and specialisation
The change from broadcast to narrowcast, and the increasing availability of information and evaluation about what is available, places an extra premium on customer-perceived quality for business success, and favours high-quality specialist suppliers.

Downsizing the corporation
As it becomes increasingly difficult to excel in many diverse businesses, large conglomerates are splitting off peripheral businesses to define their core businesses; success will go to many agile small competitors.

Virtual companies
Communication technologies and applications (such as e-mail and EDI) facilitate the rapid assembly of temporary consortia, of several 'best of breed' specialists, to compete successfully for large contracts against old-style groupings of units which happen to be under the same corporate umbrella.

Internationalism
As more nations become competitive in knowledge industries (eg in the Pacific rim, and ex-communist countries), as international communications networks improve, and as legislation erodes national barriers to trade (eg CEC) most businesses face ever-growing competition from overseas.

Constant change
The factors leading to competitive advantage are becoming progressively less related to capital and massive resources (eg to buy customers' attention) and more related to knowledge - knowledge of customer preferences and new ways to satisfy them, which is short-lived and resides in the minds of key staff. Therefore competitive advantage is becoming more evanescent, with a shorter lifecycle, which in turn implies that company lifecycles are shorter. They are forced more often into the high-risk venture of reinventing themselves by radical business process reengineering. Some succeed, and others fail, but the result in any case is change. Mergers, acquisitions and restructuring become more frequent, and there is less job security.

The rate at which these changes will progress over the next five years depends largely on the commercial success of 'narrowcast' information dissemination over the Internet and what follows it (or what the Net evolves into). We are currently at a watershed with many companies, large and small, dipping a toe into these waters, but still with some scepticism over whether and when 'doing business over the Net' will become a large-scale reality. Issues of information security, payment mechanisms, available bandwidth and penetration of the home market are seen as possible inhibitors. In response to these queries it is possible to say that:

- Technical solutions to the problem of payment mechanisms exist already, and are being trialled by a number of organisations such as Barclay Square; it should only take a short time for one or two of these solutions to become de facto leaders which are widely accepted and used.

- Security is mainly not a technical problem, but a matter of how much organisations are prepared to pay (in setting up and using the necessary mechanisms) for security. Society will tolerate less-than-perfect security over the Internet, as it does for other systems (computer-based or not) in return for the commercial benefits.

- New applications are proliferating which hog bandwidth, and degrade Net performance for all users. The commercial structures for information transmission will adapt themselves so that these services have somehow to pay more for the bandwidth they consume; but the rapid increase in available bandwidth implies that these cost penalties will not be severe, and will not inhibit the growth of Net use by these services.

- In the UK currently relatively few homes have Internet access, so services aimed at the home have a small market. It is not yet clear whether domestic penetration will come via a set-top box in the living room, or via a PC in the study; but there seems little doubt that, following the United States, the home market will have been opened up in some manner or other within the next five years.

In other words, these inhibitors will all be surmounted, leading to a high level of business over the Net; in the year 2000 an order of 10% of GDP may involve transactions over the Internet or its successors.

It is hard to guess which business areas will lead this expansion; but current indications are that serious uses of the Internet occur where people require easy access to large volumes of high-quality information (as, for instance, in academic research publishing - an area of intense Internet activity, where the demise of printed journals over the next five years has been predicted). Other leading business applications will be driven by a public appetite for large amounts of high-quality (and probably volatile) information.

21.3 How Information Technology will change the way people work

There are a number of generic applications of IT, which we are now seeing in their early forms, whose use will increase rapidly over the next five years. While in the seventies and eighties IT was used mainly in the support of routine clerical work, today it supports not only that but also an increasing range of knowledge workers - whose role is becoming more central to company success because of the changes noted in the previous section. These generic applications are:

Group working and workflow (asynchronous team applications)

The word 'asynchronous' means that an IT system supports two or more people in some task or job without requiring them to both be at a terminal at the same time; the archetypal asynchronous application is e-mail. Two groups of applications follow from this:

1. Lotus Notes is a leading example of a number of products for group working support which extend e-mail to allow distributed teams to work together in many different ways - defining their own workflows, conferencing and sharing databases, mixing and matching these for the job in hand. Notes excels in supporting creative, ad hoc working teams of knowledge workers, in ways they define for themselves.
2. More formalised, structured Workflow systems support more routine processing such as insurance claims through a succession of stages - typically in ways which are defined for the workers by others.

Videoconferencing and shared documents (synchronous team applications)

Many organisations now have enough network bandwidth and PC power on the desk to support desktop videoconferencing, and this is becoming more than a conference phone call where you can see the other peoples' faces. Tools are available to enable participants to share documents (text, spreadsheets, diagrams) and to modify them in real time, and to facilitate group interactions.

Paper reduction

It is easy to scoff at predictions of the paperless office, and many commentators have done so; up to the present, they seem to have been justified. However, a number of straightforward IT inconvenience factors which have inhibited the replacement of paper are now being rapidly eroded by technology:

● The cost of scanning
Most incoming paper gets put through a copier at some stage. If it could be scanned into electronic form just as easily (as will soon be the case) then organisations are able to 'go paperless', if they wish to, in spite of incoming paper documents from others.

● Document quality
Computer screens currently do not show a document with as good print quality as a well-printed page - a difference which is steadily diminishing.

Reading and annotating documents

At present we read electronic documents through a word processor, which is not designed for the purpose. A software tool which enables us to easily flip through a document, annotate it by pen or voice, and to search for phrases or our own annotations, can be easily built and will be when the market demands it.

Against these rapidly diminishing disadvantages, the computer has some major advantages:
(a) the ability to search documents by keyword;
(b) the use of hypertext structures to escape the one-dimensionality of paper, allowing different readers to read a document to different levels of detail, and to follow specific trails or tailor-made trails through a document;
(c) the ability to access over a network, or carry in a laptop, large amounts of information; today's laptops can carry on their hard disks the equivalent of half a ton of paper;
(d) in the near future, the ability to make on-line translation or précis of documents.

The advantage (c) is likely to prove decisive for mobile knowledge workers, to liberate them from bulging and inadequate brief-cases. Another factor which will hasten the change is the availability of increasing amounts of high-quality information over the Internet - knowing that this information is readily available diminishes the motivation to carry it around yourself in paper form, and helps to wean us away from paper information. So although the paperless office is not in evidence now, and may never occur in its extreme form, we can expect that in the next five years the proportion of business information which is tied to paper will rapidly diminish.

Flexible working and telecommuting
Already many organisations are finding that 'hot-desking' can save them significant costs in building space and travel time; it is largely the computer support of mobile workers which is making this possible. Only if the bulk of one's working information is available over the corporate network, or is portable in a laptop, is hot-desking a real possibility. This also makes possible an increased amount of working from home. Although very few people will want to work completely from home, missing the social contact inherent in an office, nevertheless part-time home working will be positive and effective for many.

The Information Highway
Although the public business uses of the Information Highway have so far made only very limited progress (see previous section) many corporations are making increasing use of Internet-type technologies (eg hypertext repositories and browsers) for the management and dissemination of their own internal corporate information. Since most people spend more time communicating within their own organisation than communicating across businesses, this may have a larger impact on work practices than the public uses of the information highway.

It would perhaps be foolish to try to predict just what mix of Internet technologies, EDI, conferencing and group working applications will drive the growth of business-to-business traffic over public networks; but surely some of these developments will drive it rapidly over the next five years.

Agent-based systems
An agent is some more-or-less 'intelligent' piece of software (possibly using AI techniques) which acts autonomously on behalf of a person or business over public networks and services, to procure a result for them such as a piece of information or a purchase. It has been said that the success of an agent will be gauged not by what it can do,

but by how well it can explain itself; while it is a fairly straightforward technical problem to build certain kinds of functionality into a software agent, it is much harder to do it so that occasional users (with no deep understanding of the underlying technology) come to trust the agent to do just what they want, and are able to instruct it to do so. For this reason alone the success of agent-based systems over the next 5-10 years is by no means guaranteed; we may look back then and find agents have failed a basic usability test.

Continuous business process re-engineering
As the pace of business change increases, and as the software tools and building blocks for constructing new business applications improve, it becomes easier, and more necessary, and quicker, to build new processes supported by IT which radically change the way organisations work. However, it also becomes harder and harder to predict the impact of these new business processes on the culture and motivation of an organisation. Often companies will not get it right first time, and will have to keep experimenting until they do get it right, or fail as companies. Employees must expect the continual reconfiguration of their jobs.

User-defined applications
The reconfiguration of jobs will not always be imposed from outside, or from the centre of the business; often it will be decided locally by departments or small teams. Tools such as spreadsheets and Lotus Notes, and architectures such as OLE2 and OpenDoc, make it increasingly easy for local departments and groups of workers to reconfigure computing power to do the jobs they want it to do, in support of their own work. Their job success will then depend on their ability to build such mini-systems, as well as their ability to do the job itself. The corporate IT role is then to provide the IT and communications infrastructure, and the standards, to make this possible.

Training and help systems
With the increasing volatility of work, the ability to rapidly re-train for new jobs becomes more important. Computer-based tools (CBT) will be used not only to provide automatic training (via the rapidly improving CBT technology, using multi-media techniques) but also to provide on-the-job help when required, to put novices in touch with experts who can help them, and to share experience.

21.4 Technology enablers

This section briefly describes some of the key technologies (hardware and software) which will underpin the application developments previously described.

Mobile computing

The laptop computer will continue its evolutionary improvement and increased take-up, until it becomes an expected entitlement with most jobs, just like the telephone. With increasingly high-quality A4-size colour screens, inbuilt networking capability, and inbuilt pen and voice interfaces, it will come to replace not only the briefcase but also the notebook taken into meetings. Convenience software (for document browsing, communication and note-taking), not requiring any great advances in software technology, will make today's desktop software look archaic and clunky. There will be an interesting convergence or competition between this powerful device and the cellular telephone.

High-performance networks

While computer processing power and storage have made steady increases with each decade, network bandwidth has until recently lagged behind - but is now poised to make a dramatic leap of 1000 times bandwidth over this decade, with the advent of asynchronous transfer mode (ATM) networks. Hardware routing of small packets enables ATM networks to carry hundreds of megabits bandwidth, with the very small latencies needed for simultaneous data, voice and video traffic. This step-function change will transform corporate IT architectures (for instance, enabling text, data and video to be centralised in large repositories with acceptable performance) and will transform the way businesses use information. It will avert the choking of the Internet.

Object orientation

This fashionable phrase describes not a cure-all, but a grouping together of several techniques (such as modularity, encapsulation, and inheritance) which are now a necessary part of the intellectual toolkit needed to build today's complex, evolving, user-centred software-based systems. Now that users expect to be in control of the computer (rather than the other way round, as was the case 15 years ago), the interface must present users with a set of objects (eg documents) with consistent behaviour, so that they can choose what to do with which object, rather than be directed by prompts from the computer. A high degree of encapsulation enables designers to understand objects in terms of what they do, not the internal mechanisms by which they do it; and so designers can compose objects together rapidly to build powerful systems with minimal effort. Encapsulation also enables the emergence of an open market in software components (bought and sold on the basis of their visible functions, not their internals), which will drive down the cost of good software components; for instance there is now a market for OpenDoc components over the Internet.

However, the take-up of object orientation is not a smooth process of steady improvement. Often, as in other aspects of software, commercial pressures lead to the establishment of de facto standards such as C++ and OLE2, and the inertia of the standard retards progress for several years.

In this respect, two interesting battles for the market are currently taking place: OLE2 versus DSOM/OpenDoc and Object-oriented databases (ODBMS) versus extended relational databases (RDBMS). ODBMS have attracted a lot of interest, but may have failed to reach industrial strength (in terms of support for large databases, recovery, multi-user, etc.; and market penetration) in their window of opportunity. There are signs that ODBMS will be permanently confined to a niche around applications such as CAD/CAM.

New interfaces

To rapidly survey the status of several new interface technologies:

(a) Speech

We are fast approaching the point where the raw technology of speech recognition - extracting phonemes and words from a sound signal - is at its technological limit, close to human performance (computer recognition of isolated words is highly error-prone). However, the great challenge is to link speech recognition with natural language understanding and knowledge of the meaning and context, to give human-like levels of speech understanding. The market has recently seen the launch of a number of software products that claim to offer accurate recognition of continuous speech.

Meanwhile, the use of speech interfaces will grow modestly in a number of niche applications - dictation, command interfaces in 'hands-free' work situations and over the telephone, and recording meetings for archive and later search by keyword. A fundamental inhibitor is that people do not like to be seen talking to a machine.

(b) Handwriting recognition

Some early handwriting recognisers were a false start with very poor usability, and may have set back user acceptance of the technology by several years. This is a shame, because the underlying technical problems are not insoluble; the real challenge is in the user interface, to ensure first that handwriting offers a real benefit to the user for his/her task (so he/she is prepared to persevere, to train the machine and so on) and second that recognition failures are handled gracefully and easily. All this can be done without rocket science, and will be done, as soon as the appropriate platforms (eg tomorrow's laptops) and applications are identified.

(c) Virtual reality

Today, VR interfaces still have un-commercial, researchy, games-machine associations, and little work has been done to explore their real benefits and uses for commercial applications. However, this is changing rapidly for two reasons: first, cable and telephone companies see the potential of VR interfaces over the television for video-on-demand, shopping mall and other interactive TV applications; and second, VR browsers and definition languages (such as VRML) will soon be widely and cheaply available on the Internet. These will produce an explosion of experimentation in VR interfaces, which should rapidly establish what they are really good for.

For many people, a spatial/navigational metaphor is a very effective way to index memory ("what did I do when I was last here?"), so VR interfaces have great potential to help people cope with possible information overload. However, VR landscapes which are populated just with simple geometric shapes (cones, rectangles, etc.) soon seem artificial and fatiguing; the costs of designing truly congenial VR interfaces are probably much greater than most software developers realise. If VR becomes a 3-D version of Powerpoint clip art

(the cliché of many business presentations) little will have been achieved.

(d) Optical character recognition

This is something of a Cinderella amongst computer interfaces - it has been around for many years, is potentially very useful doing a mundane task (to convert paper-based information into easily accessible, indexed, portable computer form) and yet is little appreciated or used. Why is this? Partly because document scanning is still tedious (much slower than copying a document, although it need not be) and partly because OCR software is error-prone and requires hand-steering to pick out the required text. These, as for handwriting recognition, are low-tech usability issues rather than rocket science; they will probably be solved within the next few years, as the demand for paper reduction and information portability increases.

To summarise on all these new interface technologies: the issues holding them back are more ones of usability, usefulness for specific tasks, engineering and cost-effectiveness, rather than any fundamental technology barriers.

Rapid development toolkits

The history of computing has in one sense been a history of ever higher and higher-level languages, to express problems in more user-oriented, application-specific terms, as opposed to machine-oriented terms. Over the years, this change - from machine code to assembler code to high-level languages to fourth generation languages - has given dramatic increases in productivity and in the quality of systems developed; and there is no sign of an end to this trend. Its latest incarnation - effectively its fifth generation - is in the so-called rapid development toolkits, which themselves can be arranged into three 'mini-generations':

● 1st mini-generation
Tools such as early versions of Visual Basic and Powerbuilder, which give very high productivity, and often a fairly good user interface, on restricted applications; but which may prove difficult to manage on larger endeavours.

● 2nd mini-generation
Tools such as Uniface, Informix New Era, and Borland's Delphi, which typically incorporate rather more 'true' object orientation, or are

based on a better formalised 3-layer client-server model, to give better separation of concerns, evolvability and manageability for large projects.

● 3rd mini-generation
Toolkits which embody full distributed object technology, and create a wide market in cheaply available objects for all sorts of specialist applications. This generation is now becoming available through developments such as Taligent, Next Step OpenDoc, and integrated Web-aware toolkits typified by Microsoft Visual Studio.

All of these are to be welcomed, and they undoubtedly point to the future shape of software development. However, they also highlight new problems of managing the development process, because they encourage constant interaction between developers and users, and make prototyping and iteration an essential part of the process. This interactive, iterative development process is a necessity for the rapid, evolutionary style of business process change which is mandated by commercial pressures on user organisations (section 21.2); but it is harder to manage than the traditional waterfall development model, and it may take us longer to master these software management problems than to master the new technologies themselves. The public-domain Dynamic Systems Development Method (DSDM) provides probably the best available framework for managing these issues.

21.5 Blocking factors

Advances in technology do not alter some underlying business realities which impede progress. Some of these are:

Standards Wars
Progress in the application of IT depends on the widespread acceptance of certain standards for interworking of hardware, software and information. Simple, successful standards such as the EDI standards are of great business benefit. However, the progress of standardisation is often not so straightforward - either because the topics for standardisation are so complex that standards committees are incapable of solving all the problems and interactions which they raise (as, for instance in the Open Systems standardisation efforts) or because two or more

candidate standards both have heavy commercial backing. The industry may be subject to years of uncertainty and extra costs, and the eventual winner may well not be the candidate of greatest merit.

The past few years have seen de facto standards battles around desktop operating systems (DOS/Windows vs. OS/2) and integrated office application suites (Microsoft Office versus several others). There are signs that these areas are no longer the main battlefield, but that the important struggles will be in:

(a) Client-server application systems
Standards for application distribution, transaction management, recovery, security, etc - the application end of the Open Systems standardisation issues.

(b) Distributed middleware
To support both the extension of desktop office applications into group working support (Lotus Notes versus Microsoft Exchange; DSOM/OpenDoc versus OLE2).

The two areas are, of course, closely related; and the outcome will determine how tomorrow's object-oriented, group working distributed applications are built.

Past standards battles have been slow titanic struggles, as major industry players laboured over years to develop large products which embodied their candidates - announcing and releasing products prematurely to secure a position, then failing to deliver them. Users were frequently disappointed with the results, but resigned to accepting the dominant player's offering.

Two developments are helping to free up this unsatisfactory situation. First, object orientation means that applications - including standard desktop applications such as word processing and spreadsheets - are increasingly composed of middle-sized objects rather than monolithic blocks of software, opening up a freer market for these objects. Second, the Internet serves both as a public forum for standards discussions (no longer restricted to standards committees behind closed doors) and as a rapid vehicle to propagate, and evaluate, cheap candidate standards.

Companies such as Netscape can sell their products cheaply, distributing free evaluation copies over the Net to reach large markets quickly, and succeed or fail rapidly. This freeing up of markets must benefit users.

The difficulty of large integration projects

While better development tools and the market for objects will continue to make system development easier, companies still demand new applications which stretch the technology of the day to its limits, requiring over-sized project teams and unrealistic timescales. Such large projects often fail, and an analysis of the causes of failure reveals three key factors of a timeless, technology-independent nature:

(1) fluctuating and conflicting requirements;
(2) the thin spread of application domain knowledge;
(3) communication and co-ordination difficulties.

Advances in technology will do little to solve these problems; so we can expect that businesses will continue to initiate large, bet-the-business, system development projects in order to remain competitive, and that many of them will fail, for these reasons. Increasingly, project failure will lead to company failure.

Earthquakes

The progress of IT and its applications should not be expected to be an unalloyed, smooth progression into an ever-improving future. Sometimes apparent progress may in fact be building up 'sub-terranean' pressures and tensions, which from time to time release themselves with catastrophic consequences, leading to a setback for both the IT industry and its users. This can happen if, in some area of public concern, such as system security or safety, the standards applied in building IT systems are insidiously relaxed, until a large system fails, causing headlines, lawsuits, and then over-restrictive, ill-considered legislation. A possible model for this kind of 'earthquake' and the resulting setbacks is the history of the nuclear industry following the Chernobyl and Three Mile Island incidents.

In a safety context, this might involve a disaster claiming many lives, in which poor standards of IT were implicated, leading to laws restricting the use of IT for safety-related systems; laws which also outlaw applications where IT can

clearly improve system safety. For security instead of safety, substitute headline financial losses or abuses of personal privacy.

In all these areas, IT systems are steadily becoming more complex, and our dependence on those systems is increasing; commercial pressures on the sponsors and developers of those systems lead to compressed timescales and budgets in which proper attention to safety and security issues can easily be bypassed. The possibility of a resulting earthquake and retrenchment should not be neglected.

System and network management

Many organisations are coming to realise the large hidden costs of managing their networks and distributed applications across thousands of desktop computers. Market penetration of laptops makes this management problem yet harder, by increasing user autonomy. It seems that from today's partial solutions (eg the OpenView platform; SMS) we have several years of commercial evolution to go through before standard and effective solutions are commonplace; in the meantime, the resulting costs and difficulties will act as an inhibitor.

21.6 Specific topics

Three specific technology topics were identified by BRE as being of particular interest. I shall here summarise a view on each of these topics, cross-referring to other topics covered elsewhere in this chapter, as appropriate.

● Ease of access to data

Data generally takes the form of structured data, for which relational database systems (RDBMS) will continue to dominate for the foreseeable future, but increasingly will also take the form of less-structured text and multimedia (eg video, sound) information. For the latter, Internet technologies for browsing and storage are rapidly becoming dominant, and the Internet itself is establishing a public market for many sources of this information. Mobile computing technologies (laptop and pen computers; PCMCIA access cards; cellular radio) are increasing the ease of practical access to both public and corporate information of structured and unstructured kinds; while new user interfaces (speech/language, pen, VR) have few technology hurdles to overcome, but need to solve many practical usability problems. User agent technology has some promise to enhance access to information, but may well fail a usability test over the next few years. For more structured access in the course of defined business processes, Rapid Application Development tools are bringing about major improvements.

In summary, providing easy access to information is a key aim of information technology; over the next few years it will steadily enhance its ability to do so.

● Security of data

Security of data is largely not a technical problem - the technical means to defeat hackers and intruders are available - but an economic problem of how much organisations and the public are prepared to pay (particularly in the cost of more complex security operating procedures) to avoid the breaches. This depends on a largely informal estimation of the costs of breaches - an estimate which may well change following some well publicised disaster. Use of formal methods to define and prove security policies will become a mature technique, for a few high-security niches. Smart cards and biometrics will also find increasing use. The security risks of the information highway have been initially over-estimated; the technologies of firewalls, passwords, payment, and the use of public-key encryption will rapidly settle down to a more-or-less satisfactory consensus, with occasional scare stories still disturbing this situation.

In summary, the uneasy balance between the continual costs of providing proper security of data, and the sporadic costs of not having it, will continue over the next few years much as it has in the recent past.

● Storage space and data compression

Recent years have seen a steady decline in the cost, and bulk, of information storage at all levels of the storage hierarchy (random access memory with microsecond access time, bulk storage with millisecond access time, and archive storage). There is no sign of this trend stopping, with disc storage continuing to improve and new storage media continuing to appear, populating new regions of a descending price/latency curve. For instance, writeable CDs of 10 gigabyte capacity will soon be available, while tape stores with terabyte capacity are also available.

How is this matched by increases in demand? Although one might expect a Parkinsonian increase of demand to fill the available capacity, there are signs that demand may saturate before supply does, so that information storage will become a diminishing proportion of the costs of IT. One of these signs is the advent of ATM networks, which make it more practical to store large amounts of information centrally without heavy duplication, as network latency and capacity are no longer a serious bar to retrieving the information rapidly. The other is the maturation of compression technology and standards such as MPEG and fractal compression, (mainly because processing power is now adequate to de-compress on the fly in most PCs), so that video, for instance, is no longer prohibitive.

Therefore it seems likely that the supply of information storage will steadily outpace the demand; we shall be easily able to store all the information we can generate.

21.7 Conclusions

We can draw some of these considerations together by sketching a picture of a knowledge worker in some advanced sector of the economy in the early part of the new Milennium.

He/she will have a slim laptop computer, the size of an A4 pad and 1-inch thick, which is his/her principal working tool. It can be used with a pen interface to unobtrusively take notes in a meeting, deciphering the handwriting, formatting and indexing the information for later use; it connects automatically to corporate and public networks by cellular radio or infra-red link in most places - office, home or airport lounge. It actively sifts a mass of incoming and available information, such as Internet sources, to present information of current interest to its user. It has simple but effective document browsing and presentation tools, making electronic documents more congenial than paper. It may even have a built-in camera and microphone for on-the-fly conferencing, using widely available meeting support and document sharing tools.

This knowledge worker will be part of a shifting matrix of transient teams formed for specific tasks out of his/her own company and other small, agile collaborators. Standards and Net-available building blocks enable these teams to pull together common group working tools, and to configure them rapidly to support the processes designed by each team for itself. He/she spends 30% of his /her time in a base office, where he/she has no permanent desk but uses a range of purpose-designed meeting, group working and social facilities; the quality of this office is one of the reasons he/she stays with this company (although the company does not own the office; along with several others, it rents space and facilities on a short-term basis and will 'trade up' when better ones become available). He/she works 40% at home, and 30% on the premises of his/her clients and collaborators; although increasing uptake of advanced high quality videoconferencing facilities is by now diminishing the need for travel.

Bibliography and appendices

Part 1

Part 2

Part 3

Part 4

Part 5

Bibliography and appendices

Bibliography

Franklin Becker. *The Ecology of New Ways of Working: Non-Territorial Offices.* Industrial Development, January/February 1993, vol. 162, no. 1, pp. 1-6.

BRE. *People and lighting controls. Information Paper* IP6/96. Garston, CRC, 1996.

BRECSU. *A series of office case studies, energy consumption guides, and information reports.* BRE, Garston.

BRECSU. *Avoiding or minimising the use of air-conditioning.* GIR 31. BRE, Garston,1995.

W T Bordass,A K R Bromley and A J Leamon. *Comfort, control and energy efficiency in offices.* Information Paper IP3/95. Garston, CRC, 1995.

Michael Brill. *Now offices, No offices, New offices...* Teknion, 1994.

Kate Button. *'New Wave' rolls over corporate America.* Management Consultancy, June 1993.

CIBSE. *Natural ventilation in non-domestic buildings.* Applications Manual AM10:1997.

Paul Cornell, Robert Luchetti, Lisbeth A Mack and Gary M Olson. *CSCW: Evolution and Status of Computer Supported Cooperative Work.* Symposium of the Human Factors Society, Denver, Colorado, August 1989.

Peter F Drucker. *The New Society of Organizations.* Harvard Business Review, Sept-October, 1992.

John J Dues. *Andersen Consulting's Office Program for Managers Employs Just-in-Time concepts,* Industrial Development, September/October 1992, no.2, pp. 6-9.

Francis Duffy. *The New Office.* Conran Octopus, 1997.

Francis Duffy and J Tanis. *A vision of the new workplace.* In Industrial Development section, April 1993.

Francis Duffy, Andrew Laing and Vic Crisp. *The Responsible Workplace.* Butterworth Architecture, London 1993.

Francis Duffy. *The Changing Workplace.* Phaidon, 1992.

Martin P Dugan. *Workstation Options to Encourage Innovation and Productivity.* Industrial Development, March/April 1992, vol. 161, no. 2 pp. 1-5.

Richard Florida. *The New Industrial Revolution.* Futures, July August, 1991

R Grenier and G Metes. *Enterprise networking, working together apart.* Digital Press, 1992.

Charles Handy. *The future of work.* Oxford and New York, 1985.

Robert J Hiller. *The Future Workplace: Flexible, Adaptable, and Individual.* Industrial Development, March/April 1992, vol. 161, no. 2 pp 6-7.

R Johansen at al. *Leading business teams, how teams can use technology and group process tools to enhance performance.* Addison Wesley Publishing company, 1991.

P J Littlefair. *Designing with innovative daylighting.* BR305. Garston, CRC, 1996.

M H Lyons, P Cochrane and K Fisher. *Telecommuting in the 21st Century.* Computing Control Engineering Journal, August 1993.

W Miller and L Bloomquist. *Trends that affect the design of furniture.* Paper from conference on Productivity in knowledge intensive organisations, Grand Rapids, Michigan, 1992.

G J Raw (ed). *A questionnaire for studies of sick building syndrome.* BRE, 1995.

Robert Reich. *The Work of Nations: Preparing ourselves for 21st century capitalism.* Alfred A. Knopf, New York, 1991.

Philip J Stone and Robert Luchetti. *Your Office is Where You Are.* Harvard Business Review, March-April, 1985.

Philip J Stone and Robert Luchetti. *Creating Offices that Support Cooperation and Teamwork.* San Francisco, August 14, 1990.

L Tesler. *Networked computing in the 1990s.* Scientific American, September 1991.

Timothy H Walker. *Designing Work Environments that Promote Corporate Productivity.* Industrial Development, March/April, 1992, vol. 161, no. 2, pp. 8-10.

M Weiser. *The computer for the 21st Century.* Scientific American, September, 1991.

Martha Whitaker. *The future of work and the workplace: less monolithic, more pluralistic.* Industrial Development, September/October 1992, vol. 161, no. 5, pp. 1-5.

Shoshanna Zuboff. *In the age of the smart machine, the future of work and power.* London, 1990.

Appendix A

HVAC system descriptions and definitions

1 Window ventilation and radiator perimeter heating

Air enters and leaves the building via a combination of opening windows and trickle ventilators to provide ventilation throughout the year, and to dispel excess heat when required. The radiator system provides heating during the winter. The indoor temperature is always higher than the outside temperature. In winter ventilation with cold outdoor air can cause discomforting draughts. At any time of the year air entering through windows is unfiltered and carries with it any fumes and contaminants present in the outdoor air. Similarly, open windows provide a direct route for outdoor noise intrusion to the office space. The effectiveness of natural ventilation is limited in deep plan spaces.

2 Window facade ventilation and radiator perimeter heating

This is similar to 1 but has an extra facade located 600 mm to 1m outside the window wall. The void between the inner and outer facades is sectionalised with one devoted to bringing air into each room at low level and the other to collecting and dispelling 'spent' air from high level in each room. The arrangement improves the effectiveness of the ventilation and reduces the adverse effects of wind and outdoor noise. As with window ventilation, the system affords no means of filtering the air supply.

3 Mechanical extract ventilation, window supply and radiator heating

This is similar to systems 1 and 2, but some ventilation is assured as the 'spent' room air is positively removed by means of fans which induce some outside air to enter via the windows regardless of the prevailing weather.

4 Mechanical supply and extract ventilation with radiator heating

This is a development of system 3. Outdoor air is now also positively brought into the room from a central air handling unit which is normally equipped with a supply and extract fan, air filters and heater to temper the supply air in cold weather. The air supply is not however cooled.

5 Mechanical displacement ventilation with radiator heating

Displacement ventilation involves the introduction of a low velocity air stream at low level within the space, its temperature being only slightly below the desired room temperature. The supply air forms a pool of cool air in the lower part of the occupied space. Internal heat sources such as people or equipment warm the air surrounding them to create convective plumes which entrain air from this cool pool and cause an upward movement. This warm air rises and forms a layer at the ceiling where it is removed by a high level mechanical extract system. The effect of the convective plumes is not only to cool but also to remove contaminants from the breathing zone as the air is drawn over the occupants. Dehumidification of the supply air may be required in summer to maintain a suitable humidity within the space.

6 Mechanical displacement ventilation with static heating and cooling

This is a development of system 5 with additional static cooling provided actively by chilled ceiling panels or beams to meet local cooling requirements. The static cooling panels are fed with lightly cooled water provided by a central chiller. Warming is also by static means, usually in the form of perimeter radiators.

7 Ventilating chill/heat beams

This system involves providing a supply of lightly cooled outdoor air from a central air handling unit to long 'beam like' metal boxes hung from the ceiling. These can be exposed or concealed. The air supply out of these ventilating beams is arranged in order to induce air from the room through finned beams concealed within the boxes. Hot or cold water is circulated through the finned beams to heat or cool the air as required.

8 Four-pipe fan coil units with central ventilation

This is a conventional form of air conditioning. Fans coils are boxes containing a fan, air heating and cooling coils, and an air filter. The coils are served with hot and cold water from central boilers and chiller plant. Room air is continually circulated through them, being heated or cooled as required. The units are usually concealed in ceiling voids but can be floor mounted. Fresh air is normally delivered separately to the room from a central air handling unit where it is filtered and tempered, although it is possible for it to be supplied directly through units standing adjacent to an external wall.

9 ATM zonal air conditioning

Air treatment modules (ATMs) are large floor standing boxes (usually housed in purpose built cupboards in the office) which contain a number of fan coils. They can also be smaller individual units which are housed in distributed plant rooms. In both cases air is conveyed between the ATM and the rooms it serves through flexible ducting concealed in the ceiling void. Changes in room partitioning can be accommodated by changing this flexible duct configuration. The ATM can be accessed for maintenance without entering the office space. Outdoor air is supplied through the ATM to rooms usually from a central air handling unit, as with conventional fan coils.

10 Terminal heat pump with central ventilation

Terminal heat pump units are arranged in a manner very similar to the fan coil units of system 8. In this case however heating and cooling of the air supply is achieved by a small reversible heat pump built into each unit. The heat pump is actually a refrigerant circuit that either presents its evaporator to the airstream to cool it, or its condenser to heat it. Surplus heating or cooling produced by the heat pump is dispelled to a tepid water ring main circulating through all the units. This can balance energy use between rooms that are on opposing heating and cooling cycles as can occur for some periods of the year. When the circulating water system becomes too cold it is warmed by a central boiler system. When it is too hot central chiller plant is brought into operation.

11 VAV air conditioning with radiator perimeter heating

This is a conventional central air conditioning system having a mixture of outdoor and recirculating air which is filtered and cooled at a central air handling unit, from whence it is ducted to the rooms. The flow of cold air delivered into each room is varied by a local variable air volume (VAV) terminal box - essentially a modulating air damper - to match the cooling needs of the room. The main fans are controlled to adjust the overall air flow to the building based on the consensus of all the terminal boxes' demands for air. The VAV boxes and their ductwork are concealed in ceiling voids.

12 VAV air conditioning with terminal re-heat

This is similar to system 11 but with a local heater in each VAV terminal providing the warming instead of a radiator system.

13 Fan assisted terminal VAV

In this case a fan is added into each VAV terminal to mix circulating room air with the central ducted variable flow air supply. The fan assists in maintaining a constant air flow volume and avoids some of the problems that can arise with basic VAV systems when a minimal cooling requirement can lead to problems in maintaining a good air distribution pattern.

14 Low temperature air fan assisted terminal VAV

This is a development of system 13 where air from the central plant VAV system is delivered at 8-10°C or less as opposed to 12-14°C for traditional VAV systems . As less air is needed to convey a given quantity of cooling this can permit smaller ducts and hence requires less service space. The low temperature air is often cooled by an ice store in conjunction with a chiller which is operated night and day to either make ice for the following day, or to supplement the cooling available from the ice. In this way the size of the refrigeration plant can be made far smaller than for alternative forms of air conditioning system.

15 Induction unit air conditioning

Induction unit air conditioning comprises a series of boxes sited in ceiling voids or on walls, connected to a high pressure supply air system from a central air handling unit. This main air supply is delivered through nozzles in the induction unit which has the effect of inducing air from the room into the unit. Here it combines with the main supply and the two air streams are heated or cooled by a coil served with hot or cold water produced by central plant.

16 Dual duct air conditioning (constant volume)

Dual duct is a conventional central air conditioning system. Separate cold and warm air ducts carry a mixture of filtered outdoor and recirculated air to each room where the two air streams are blended by modulating dampers in purpose made enclosures and delivered into the room.

17 VRF cooling system

This is a relatively new system which operates on the principle of the heat pump. Several room units are connected directly to a single outdoor refrigeration unit. The refrigerant flow rate to each unit can be varied using a variable speed compressor in response to cooling requirements. The units can be switched to heating or cooling mode as required and it is possible with some systems to have a number of units operating in heating mode whilst others are cooling, so that there is the potential to balance heating and cooling as in system 10.

18 Hollow core ventilation system

This system makes use of the building fabric as a means of transporting ventilation supply air. A low powered fan is used to drive air through an 's' shaped pathway formed using three of the cores of a modified hollow core concrete floor module. A hole drilled in the lower surface of the floor module allows air to be expelled into the room below through ceiling grilles. 'Spent' air may be removed from the room through an exhaust air duct served by another fan or by means of natural ventilation. There is a minimal need for mechanical cooling in this system (although it can be assisted by supplementary cooling). Air supply rates are typical of ventilation requirements rather than cooling requirements.

Appendix B

Occupant survey questionnaire

This questionnaire has been used exclusively within the NEW project. For details of the BRE standard questionnaire, please refer to the Bibliography.

1 Environmental comfort in winter

In this section of the questionnaire please tick one box on each scale to judge how comfortable you find your typical working conditions in winter.

1.1 Temperature in winter

1.1.1 Please rate the temperature on a typical winter's day:

Too hot	Fairly hot	Satisfactory	Fairly cold	Too cold

1.1.2 Does the temperature vary at all during the day?

Varies significantly	Moderately	Stable

1.1.3 If it varies significantly please give details:

1.2 Indoor air quality in winter

1.2.1 Please rate the humidity of the air on a typical winter's day:

Too dry	Fairly dry	Satisfactory	Fairly humid	Too humid

1.2.2 Please rate the quality of the air movement on a typical winter's day:

Too stuffy	Fairly stuffy	Satisfactory	Fairly draughty	Too draughty

1.2.3 Please rate the odour of your office on a typical winter's day:

Satisfactory	Slight odour	Very smelly

1.3 Lighting

1.3.1 Please rate the quality of the lighting at your desk on a typical winter's day:

Too dark	Fairly dark	Satisfactory	Fairly bright	Too bright

1.3.2 Please rate the lighting in the general office areas on a typical winter's day:

Too dark	Fairly dark	Satisfactory	Fairly bright	Too bright

1.3.3 Please rate the amount of unavoidable glare on computer screens that occurs on a typical winter's day:

No glare	Occasional glare	Glare 50% of time	Glare more than 50%	Continuous glare

1.3.4 Please indicate the source of the glare if it is a problem for you.

Artificial source	Natural source	Don't know

1.4 Daylighting

1.4.1 Please indicate how often it is necessary to supplement the level of daylight you get at your workplace with artificial lighting in the winter:

Never	Sometimes	Always

2 Environmental comfort in summer

In this section of the questionnaire please tick one box on each scale to judge how comfortable you find your typical working conditions in summer.

2.1 Temperature in summer

2.1.1 Please rate the temperature on a typical summer's day:

Too hot	Fairly hot	Satisfactory	Fairly cold	Too cold

2.1.2 Does the temperature vary at all during the day?

Varies significantly	Moderately	Stable

2.1.3 If it varies significantly please give details:

2.2 Indoor air quality in summer

2.2.1 Please rate the quality of the air on a typical summer's day:

Too dry	Fairly dry	Satisfactory	Fairly humid	Too humid

2.2.2 Please rate the quality of the air flow on a typical summer's day:

Too stuffy	Fairly stuffy	Satisfactory	Fairly draughty	Too draughty

2.2.3 Please rate the odour of your office on a typical summer's day:

Satisfactory	Slight odour	Very smelly

2.3 Lighting

2.3.1 Please rate the quality of the lighting at your desk on a typical summer's day:

Too dark	Fairly dark	Satisfactory	Fairly bright	Too bright

2.3.2 Please rate the lighting in the general office areas on a typical summer's day:

Too dark	Fairly dark	Satisfactory	Fairly bright	Too bright

2.3.3 Please rate the amount of unavoidable glare on computer screens that occurs on a typical summer's day:

No glare	Occasional glare	Glare 50% of time	Glare more than 50%	Continuous glare

2.3.4 Please indicate the source of the glare if it is a problem for you.

Artificial source	Natural source	Don't know

2.4 Daylighting

2.4.1 Please indicate how often it is necessary to supplement the level of daylight you get at your workplace with artificial lighting in the summer:

Never	Sometimes	Always

3   Noise

3.1   Please rate the amount of distraction you experience from your work colleagues and their activities:

No distraction	Rare distraction	Moderate distraction	A lot of distraction	Constant distraction

3.2   Please rate the amount of distraction you experience from office equipment:

No distraction	Rare distraction	Moderate distraction	A lot of distraction	Constant distraction

3.3   Please rate the amount of noise distraction you experience from the heating, ventilating/air conditioning equipment:

No distraction	Rare distraction	Moderate distraction	A lot of distraction	Constant distraction

4   Control over environmental systems

This section asks you to describe the degree of control you consider that you personally have over the environmental systems (HVAC), lighting (daylight and electric), and how this relates to your requirements.

4.1 Degree of control (eg switches, thermostats, windows, blinds)

4.1.1 Please rate the amount of control you have over the temperature in your work space:

No control	Limited control	Moderate amount	Considerable control	Full control

4.1.2 Please rate the amount of control you have over the ventilation in your work space:

No control	Limited control	Moderate amount	Considerable control	Full control

4.1.3 Please rate the amount of control you have over the artificial lighting in your work space:

No control	Limited control	Moderate amount	Considerable control	Full control

4.1.4 Please rate the amount of control you have over the shading devices in your work space:

No control	Limited control	Moderate amount	Considerable control	Full control

4.2 Frequency of control

4.2.1 Please rate how often you exercise your control over the temperature in your work space:

Never	Occasionally	Sometimes	Often	Continually

4.2.2 Please rate how often you exercise your control over the ventilation in your work space:

Never	Occasionally	Sometimes	Often	Continually

4.2.3 Please rate how often you exercise your control over the lighting in your work space:

Never	Occasionally	Sometimes	Often	Continually

4.3 Understanding of controls

4.3.1 Please rate the amount of understanding you have of the controls of the environmental systems in general:

No understanding	Very little	Some understanding	Moderate	Full understanding

4.3.2 Who explained the control operation to you?

Colleague
Technical staff
Other

4.4 Control improvements

4.4.1 Please rate how satisfied you are with the controls provided:

Not at all	Slightly	Moderately	Very satisfied	Fully satisfied

4.4.2 Please give any details of the improvements you would make if you are not fully satisfied:

5 Furniture

5.1 Please rate how suited you feel the furniture is for the needs of the workers in this office:

Not at all suited	Slightly suited	Moderate	Well suited	Fully suited

5.2 Please rate how satisfied you are with your position within the office space:

Not at all	Slightly	Moderately	Very satisfied	Fully satisfied

5.3 Please rate the extent to which you were consulted in the setting up of your workstation:

Not consulted	Moderate	Fully consulted

5.4 Please rate how adjustable your workstation is to specific tasks:

Not at all	Slightly	Moderately	Very adjustable	Fully adjustable

5.5 Please give details if relevant:

5.6   Please give any details of the improvements that could be made to your workstation to aid your performance:

5.7   Please describe the location of your work space in terms of its positioning (ie perimeter office very close to window, or central area with no natural light). If your work entails moving from one location to another please indicate the most used location as your work space.

The Building and its management

6.1   Please provide details of how the building could be improved in any way to assist you in your work:

6.2   Have you ever made any complaints about the heating, ventilation or air conditioning in your office?

6.3   If the answer to the above is yes, please provide brief details in the box below, including to whom the complaint was made:

6.4 If there has been a complaint made have you been satisfied with the speed at which your complaint has been dealt with?

Not at all	Slightly	Moderately	Very satisfied	Fully satisfied

7 Environmental issues

7.1 Do you feel that this is an environmentally friendly office?

Not at all	Slightly	Moderately	Very green	Fully green

7.2 Are you concerned about this?

Not at all	Slightly	Moderately	Very concerned	Fully concerned

7.3 Have you ever been made aware of any environmentally friendly features this building has?

Yes	No

8 In conclusion

8.1 Which three items of the list below do you feel could be most improved upon in the current building?

Summertime temperatures   Wintertime temperatures
Humidity levels   Level of daylighting
Noise   Odour
Glare   Level of electrical lighting
Opening windows   Level of user control

8.2 Taking all the environmental conditions into consideration how would you rate your office as a place to work?

Very satisfied   **Not at all satisfied**

1	2	3	4	5	6	7

Thank you for taking the time to answer our questions.

Appendix C

Cost study modelling assumptions

Key assumptions

Capital costs
Sub structure costs have been excluded from this model as these vary significantly with location.

Capital costs for the building shell and HVAC systems have been estimated using Spon's price books (Davis Langdon and Everest, *Spon's Architects' and Builders* and *Spon's Mechanical and Electrical Price Books*. E & FN Spon, 1995).

The building shell costs range from £400 - 450/sqm NIA (net internal area), while the HVAC costs range from £90-210/sqm NIA. In the context of this model Mixed Mode is assumed to mean a zoned system, hence there is an implicit reduction in the amount of HVAC plant installed compared with a fully air conditioned or comfort cooled building.

Capital costs for lighting have been estimated using Thermie Programme lighting case studies (Slater A I and Davidson P J. *Energy Efficient Lighting in Buildings*. BRECSU, OPET). Costs have been converted from ECUs at a rate of £1.21/ECU. Lighting costs within the model range from £28-63/sqm. The four lighting systems are:
- passive/fixed grid: incorporates user switching and is not easy to relocate;
- passive/variable grid: incorporates user switching but is easy to relocate by means of a track system, or has limited flexibility within a slot-in suspended ceiling;
- active/fixed grid: incorporates intelligent control such as absence detection, daylight sensing, or timed control; and is not easy to relocate;
- active/variable grid: incorporates intelligent control and is easy to relocate.

For reasons of simplicity the model assumes that suspended ceilings and raised floors are installed in all the building/HVAC system combinations. In practice a suspended ceiling will not be installed where a radiative ceiling such as Termodeck is used, whilst a raised floor may not be installed where cabling is distributed around the perimeter of the building.

Furniture specifications tend to vary within an organisation depending upon the grade or activity of the workstation occupier. Capital costs within the model are based on an operative level, being the median level of the furniture within that organisational type.

Capital and installation costs for the settings do not include the fitting of furniture around columns or other structural features which may have an adverse effect on the costs.

Maintenance
There are a number of maintenance factors which could be included in a model of this type. A typical breakdown of maintenance costs for a modern air conditioned office building (Bernard Williams Associates, *Facilities Economics*. Building Economics Bureau Ltd, 1994) would be:
- Building envelope - 25%
- Boilers and pipework - 22%
- Air conditioning plant and distribution - 22%
- Electric power supplies and distribution - 16%
- Lifts - 6%
- Scenery and settings - 5%
- Grounds - 4%.

However the maintenance of the electric power supplies, lifts and grounds do not vary significantly with the type of HVAC system selected or the work pattern being employed. Hence these fall outside the scope of this study. Maintenance costs are therefore included only for the HVAC and lighting systems (incorporating power distribution equipment but not power supply) and the scenery and settings.

Building type	Work pattern	Multiplying factor
Medium depth building	Hive	1.15
	Den	1
	Cell	1
	Club	1
Deep central core building	Hive	1.15
	Club	1.15
Atrium building	Club	1.25

Figure 133 Multiplying factors for work patterns and building types

Annual shell maintenance costs, periodic shell replacement costs, and internal and external decoration of the building fabric vary according to the intensity of the building use, and with the structural form of the building. The costs per sqm NIA have been multiplied by the factors in Figure 133 to indicate this variability.

Annual shell maintenance costs increase with the age of the building. Therefore costs range from £1.50 per sqm NIA in year 1 to £3.20 per sqm NIA in year 10. Periodic shell replacement is costed at £20 per sqm NIA in year 5 and year 10. External decoration is costed at £10 per sqm NIA in year 5 and year 10. Internal decoration is costed at £5 per sqm NIA in years 3 and 9, and at £8.50 per sqm NIA in year 6.

Figure 134 shows the maintenance costs for the HVAC systems included in the model. These are based on data from Johnson Controls's database of managed properties.

	Distributed	All air	Radiative air	Mixed mode
Hive	£10/sqm	£9/sqm	£9/sqm	£7/sqm
Den				
Club				
Cell	£12/sqm	£10/sqm	£10/sqm	£9/sqm

Figure 134 Maintenance costs for the HVAC systems included in the model

Maintenance of the building services (including the electric power supplies and lift maintenance) within modern air conditioned offices typically costs £10 - 20 per sqm of gross floor area, but may range from £4 -24/sqm for less typical installations (Energy Efficiency Office, 'Energy Efficiency in Buildings - Offices', 1991). By the time the costs for electric power supplies and lift maintenance are extracted, the costs included in the model are quite comparable. Capital replacement costs of 10% at year 5 and 20% at year 10 respectively have been included in the model for HVAC equipment.

Maintenance costs for the lighting systems are based upon operational costs. This leads to maintenance costs ranging from £0.8-1.3/sqm. No capital replacement costs have been included as the lighting systems are expected to have a 10 year life.

The following refurbishment costs have been included in the model for the scenery.

	Year 5 costs	Year 10 costs
High quality	£12/sqm	£20/sqm
Medium quality	£11/sqm	£19/sqm
Low quality	£11/sqm	£19/sqm

Figure 135 Refurbishment costs for scenery included in the model

Maintenance costs for the scenery vary according to the quality of the components installed and escalate as they age. This leads to maintenance costs ranging from £6 - 8 per sqm in year 1, and from £24 - 26 per sqm in year 10. No capital replacement costs have been included for the scenery components as they are expected to have a life of more than 10 years.

The following refurbishment costs have been included in the model for the settings.

	Year 5 costs	Year 10 costs
High quality	£12/sqm	£20/sqm
Medium quality	£10.50/sqm	£19/sqm
Low quality	£9/sqm	£17/sqm

Figure 136 Refurbishment costs for settings included in the model

With the exception of the refurbishment costs every 5 years, the settings are assumed to require no regular maintenance. Equally no capital replacement costs have been included for the setting components as they are expected to have a life of more than 10 years.

Reconfiguration costs

The costs of people churn have been excluded from this model, although an allowance for re-arrangement of HVAC systems, scenery

	Fixed grid passive	Fixed grid active	Variable grid passive	Variable grid active
Multiplier	10%	8%	1%	0.8%

Figure 137 Multiplier of capital and installation costs for lighting systems used in the model

These considerations give rise to the multipliers of the capital and installation cost for each type of lighting system shown in Figure 137.

Reconfiguration costs for scenery are based upon industry standard cost per head values. They include labour and small reconstruction costs associated with the movement of demountable partitions. The costs shown in Figure 138 are incorporated into the model.

and settings components has been made. Reconfiguration costs for HVAC systems are assumed to be approximately one third of their capital cost. During a full reconfiguration it may be necessary to move 10% of the items, but the cost of moving these items will be greater than their first installation cost. A full reconfiguration is therefore costed as:

Full installation cost x 1/3 x 0.1 x 1.05

(ie full installation cost plus 5%).

The passive lighting systems have their full capital costs distributed round the building invested in the lamps, luminaires, switches and wiring. However, in an active system, approximately 20% of the cost can be assumed to be invested in the intelligent lighting controls which are unlikely to need relocating during a reconfiguration, giving rise to a reconfiguration cost of only 80% of that of the passive systems. The model assumes a reconfiguration cost of 10% of the capital cost for a fixed grid passive system. A variable grid system is going to be significantly cheaper to reconfigure than this, a figure of 10% of the fixed grid system costs has been assumed.

	Year 3 costs	Year 6 costs	Year 9 costs
High quality	£25/sqm	£30/sqm	£30/sqm
Medium quality	£25/sqm	£30/sqm	£30/sqm
Low quality	£15/sqm	£17/sqm	£20/sqm

Figure 138 Reconfiguration costs for scenery used in the model

Settings reconfiguration costs of £5.50 per sqm in year 3, £6 per sqm in year 6 and £6.25 per sqm in year 9 have been included in the model.

Utilities costs

Utilities costs are based on Energy Efficiency Office performance yardsticks for office buildings (Energy Efficiency Office, *Energy Efficiency in Buildings - Offices*, 1991). They are charged at the rates in existence during the 3rd quarter of 1995 (gas at 1.5p per kWh and electricity at 5p per kWh).

Figure 139 shows the HVAC utilities costs included in the model.

		Cost (£/sqm)						
		Medium depth				*Deep central core*		*Atrium*
		Hive	**Den**	**Cell**	**Club**	**Hive**	**Club**	**Club**
Distributed	Electricity	20	20	17.5	17.5	20	17.5	20
All air	Electricity	10	10	8.5	8	10	8	10
	Gas	3	3	2.5	2.5	3	2.5	3
Radiative air	Electricity	8	8	6.5	6.5	8	6.5	8
	Gas	2.5	2.5	2	2	2.5	2	2.5
Mixed mode	Electricity	6.5	6.5	5	8	6.5	5	6.5
	Gas	2	2.5	2	2	2.5	2	2.5

Figure 139 HVAC utilities costs included in the model

	Cost (£/sqm)						
	Medium depth				Deep central core		Atrium
	Hive	**Den**	**Cell**	**Club**	**Hive**	**Club**	**Club**
Fixed grid passive	3.6	3.6	3	3.6	4	4	3.6
Fixed grid active	1.8	1.3	1	1.3	3	2.5	1.3
Variable grid passive	2.5	2.9	2.5	2.9	3.5	3.5	2.9
Variable grid active	1.5	0.7	0.6	0.7	2.5	2	0.7

Figure 140 Utilities costs for lighting used in the model

Assuming a cost for electricity of 5p per kWh, the utilities costs attributable to lighting are shown in Figure 140. This compares with BRECSU/Energy Efficiency Office figures (Energy Efficiency Office, *Energy Efficiency in Offices*, Best Practice Programme Energy Consumption Guide 19; Building Research Energy Conservation Support Unit, 1991) ranging from £0.60 per sqm for a naturally ventilated cellular office to £3.75 per sqm for a prestige air conditioned office.

Life cycle calculations

Net Present Value calculations are based on a 10 year cycle. A discount rate of 9% has been chosen for the costs presented in this study as it represents an accepted norm at the current time, although the model includes the flexibility to change this. Capital installation costs are represented in year 0 of the calculation whereas annual and periodic maintenance costs commence in year 1.

The costs presented in this study assume that reconfiguration of the HVAC systems, lighting systems, scenery and settings occurs three times every 10 years. This rate can be varied within the model. Reconfiguration costs of the HVAC and lighting systems have been annualised across the 10 year life cycle period. Reconfiguration costs of the scenery and settings have not been annualised.

INDEX